english in japanese

english in japanese

a selection of useful loanwords

akira miura

WEATHERHILL
New York • Tokyo

First edition, 1985
First Weatherhill edition, 1998

Published by Weatherhill, Inc.
568 Broadway, Suite 705
New York, NY 10012

First published by Yohan Publications, Inc., Tokyo, Japan

Cover design by D.S. Noble.

Library of Congress Cataloging-in-Publication Data

    Miura, Akira, 1927–
        English in Japanese: a selection of useful loanwords /
by Akira Miura.
           p.   cm.
        Includes bibliographical references and indexes.
        ISBN 0-8348-0421-2
        1. Japanese language—Foreign words and phrases—
English—Dictionaries.   I. Title
    PL684.M48   1998
    495.6'2421—dc21

                                   97-51891
                                     CIP

TABLE OF CONTENTS

Introduction

INTRODUCTION

This book is a continuation of my *English Loan-words in Japanese: A Selection* (Tuttle, '79). After the first book was published, several people wrote to me, saying they wished I had dealt with more words than I did. Hence this new volume with about as many entries as the first one.

This present volume, however, has a slightly different approach. While one of the main focuses in the first volume was on the differences between English loan-words in Japanese and their non-loan counterparts, there is more emphasis in this one on the differences between English loanwords in Japanese and the original English words. The present book also deals with many more pseudo-loans, i. e. made-in-Japan "English" words, than did the previous one. Some of these pseudo-loans are so new that they did not even exist when I was writing the first volume. This volume also offers sample sentences that include loanwords, which the first volume did not do.

Despite these differences, however, there is one big similarity between this book and the previous one: this time I again discussed only loanwords of English origin. Words derived from French and German, for example, were totally excluded except in the case of a few hybrids,

i. e. compound words that are half English and half French or German. I concentrated my attention on English loanwords merely because I wished to limit the scope of my project and not because I didn't consider loanwords from other languages worth examining.

As I was writing this time, I could not help marveling at the tremendous vigor with which the Japanese have borrowed English words or created new pseudo-loans. At the same time, however, I must confess that I sometimes felt depressed by some of the meaningless changes happening in Japanese today. What does the Japanese language gain, for example, by discarding the perfectly adequate non-loan *nejimawashi* "screwdriver" in favor of *doraibaa,* or by creating new pseudo-loans such as *raibuhausu* (lit. "live house") and *surii-saizu* (lit. "three size"), which, although composed of English words, no one but Japanese would understand anyway?

All my doubt and depression aside, however, loanwords and pseudo-loans keep flourishing. I hope my book can make a contribution, however small, towards helping the reader cope better with the confusion in which the Japanese vocabulary finds itself today.

ACCENT

Accent marks are used in this book. For example, *esukeepu* is marked *e⌐suke⌐epu.* All entry headings are thus cited with accent marks unless they are accentless. In a given entry, any loanword or any corresponding non-loan cited in that particular entry is marked when cited for the first time, but not thereafter. For the sake of simplicity, sample sentences are given without accent marks.

Japanese has a pitch accent unlike English, which has a stress accent. In Japanese words, each syllable is either high or low. If the first syllable is low, the second is always high, and if the first syllable is high, the second is always low. Loanwords, too, follow this basic rule. In this book, the mark ⌐ is used to indicate a rise in pitch, and the mark ⌐ is used to indicate a fall in pitch. The syllable followed by ⌐ is usually referred to as the accented syllable. For example, e⌐suke⌐epu, a five-syllable word, should be pronounced low-high-high-low-low, and *ke,* the last syllable before the fall in pitch, is the accented syllable. Some words are left completely unmarked, e.g. *purachina.* Unmarked words are accentless (*or* unaccented) words, i.e. words that do not have a fall in pitch. In accentless words, the first syllable is always low, but the remaining syllables are all high, and there is no fall in pitch even when the words are followed by a particle. For example, *purachina wa* is pronounced as follows:

       rachina wa
    pu

TERMINOLOGY

Loanword: Word borrowed from another language. Strictly speaking, words of Chinese origin should be designated as loanwords also, but they are usually classified as *kango* "words of Chinese origin" and not as *gairaigo* "words of foreign origin" by Japanese scholars. This book simply follows that convention. *Loanword* is sometimes shortened to *loan.*

Pseudo-loan: Word which sounds like a loan but is actually a word coined in Japan, using foreign-language elements, e.g. *raibu-hausu* (lit. live house) meaning "a coffee shop that offers live music."[1]

Non-loan: Word which is not a loanword. In this book, not only words of purely Japanese origin but also words of Chinese origin, including words coined in Japan out of *kanji,* are referred to as non-loans for the sake of convenience.

ROMANIZATION

The system of romanization used in this book may be called a modified Hepburn system. It is "modified"

---

[1] Made-in-Japan "English" words are called *wasei-eigo* (和製英語) in Japanese.

because there are a few points where the present system differs from the Hepburn romanization. In this text, katakana ン is always represented as *n*, even before *m, p,* and *b*; when *n* should be pronounced independently of the vowel that follows, an apostrophe is inserted in between, as in *kuriin'appu* "cleanup"; long vowels are indicated by doubling the vowels instead of using macrons (e.g. *aa* and *oo* instead of *ā* and *ō*) in order to facilitate accent marking, e.g. ga⌐ado. (Bibliographical data, however, are presented with macrons, because that is the most accepted practice.)

In this book, loanword compounds that correspond to hyphenated words or two or more separate words in English are hyphenated, with a few exceptions such as *pinpon* which, if written in katakana, would appear without a dot, e.g. ピンポン and not ピン・ポン (a dot would normally indicate that the original English is hyphenated or is composed of two words). Loanwords are capitalized when they correspond to capitalized words in English, except perhaps in the case of *hochikisu,* which, although derived from a person's name, is not conceived of in Japanese as a proper noun.

english in japanese

a‛chi‛ibu アチーブ (<*achieve*ment test)

Achiibu does not mean "to obtain" or "to accomplish" as does the original English word *achieve*. It is simply an abbreviation of *a‛chiibumento-te‛suto* "achievement test." Although the latter is also used, the shorter form *achiibu* is probably preferred. The achievement test was first introduced to Japanese schools in 1948 (Yoshizawa and Ishiwata, p. 18).

afu-reko アフ・レコ (lit. *af*ter *reco*rding)

Afu-reko is short for *a futaa-reko‛odingu* (lit. "after-recording"), meaning "the adding of speech, music, etc., to a film or tape recording." In English, however, the adding of sounds would be called "dubbing" or "dubbing in," and not "after-recording."

a‛ge‛en アゲーン (<again)

English *again* normally corresponds to *mata* or *moo ichi-do,* both non-loans.
(1) Mata oai-shimashoo.
       "Let's meet again."
(2) Moo ichi-do itte-kudasaimasen ka.
       "Would you mind saying that again?"
In sentences such as (1) and (2) above, *ageen* would

never be used. *Ageen* is reserved for sports which require serves, especially ping-pong. In a ping-pong match, when the score is tied at deuce for the second time, it is usually referred to as *ju⌐usu age⌐en* ("deuce again"). A very strange expression, also used in ping-pong, is *a⌐geen-wa⌐n* (lit. "again one"), meaning "one more serve." This call is used after a let serve.

A⌐ibii-ru⌐kku   アイビー・ルック   (lit. Ivy look)

Aibii-rukku refers to Ivy League-style clothing, especially men's suits. This fashion was introduced to Japan in the early '60s. *A⌐ibii-suta⌐iru* (lit. "Ivy style") is synonymous with *Aibii-rukku*.

a⌐iburoo-pe⌐nshiru   アイブロー・ペンシル
(<eyebrow pencil)

Eyebrow pencil has yielded *aiburoo-penshiru* in Japanese instead of **diburau-pe⌐nshiru*,[1] which would have been closer to the original English pronunciation. The reason is obviously that whoever introduced the eyebrow pencil mispronounced *-brow*, treating it like a romanized Japanese word. The mispronunciation has unfortunately stuck.

Eyebrow and *pencil*, when used independently, corre-

[1]An asterisk used in this book indicates incorrect or unacceptable utterances.

spond to non-loans, i.e. *ma⌐yuge* and *enpitsu,* respectively.

(1) Watashi wa mayuge (*aiburoo) ga ko-sugiru n desu.
   "My eyebrows are too bushy."

(2) Enpitsu (*penshiru) o kashite-kudasai.
   "Lend me your pencil, please."

a⌐isu-kya⌐ndee   アイス・キャ⌐ンデー   (lit. ice candy)

A flavored ice on a stick, which Americans would normally refer to as a popsicle, is called *aisu-kyandee* in Japan.

(1) Aisu-kyandee o tabe-sugiru to onaka ga itaku nari-masu yo.
   "If you eat too many popsicles, you'll get a stomach ache."

aji-bira   アジ・ビラ   (lit. *agitation bill*)

Aji-bira is a combination of *aji* (short for *a⌐jiteeshon* "agitation") and *bira* ("bill," as in *Post no bills*). The word refers to posters and fliers posted or distributed by leftists for the purpose of agitating the public.

ajipuro   アジプロ   (< *agitprop*)

Ajipuro, meaning "agitation and propaganda for the cause of communism," is often considered a Japan-made abbreviation from *a⌐jiteeshon* "agitation" and *pu⌐ropaga⌐*

nda "propaganda" (see, for example, Sanseidō, p. 14). However, Arakawa (p. 36) is probably more accurate on this in ascribing it to English *agitprop*.

a⌐ji⌐-ru アジる (<*agi*tate+Japanese *ru*)

Aji-ru "to agitate" is a combination of *aji* (short for *a⌐jite⌐eshon* "agitation") and *-ru*, a Japanese verb ending. The addition of *-ru* turns *aji* into a verb. *Aji-ru* consequently conjugates like *hairu*.

(1) Ano gakusei wa aji-ru no ga joozu da.
     "That student is good at stirring people up (lit. agitating).
(2) Taishuu o aji-ranai hoo ga ii.
     "One should not agitate the masses."
     Aji-ru refers only to agitating for political causes.

ajito アジト (<*ajit*ation point)

Ajito came into use during the Taisho era (1912-26), when the first wave of Marxism hit Japan. It refers to a secret headquarters of Communist leaders engaged in illegal activities.

Ajito is explained either as an abbreviation of English *agitation point* (Kōjien, p. 35) or as being derived from Russian *agitpunkt* (Sanseidō, p. 14).

a̒kuseru アクセル (<*accel*erator)

An automobile accelerator is *a̒kuserere̒etaa,* which is often shortened to *akuseru.* To *akuseru* is sometimes added *pedaru* to form *a̒kuseru-pe̒daru* (lit. *accel*erator *pedal*), a pseudo-loan. *Akuseru, akuserereetaa,* and *akuseru-pedaru* all refer to the same thing.

(1) A: Kono kuruma hen desu nee. Akuseru o funde mo ugokimasen yo.
        "This car is strange. Even though I'm stepping on the accelerator, it doesn't start at all."
    B: Sore wa akuseru ja arimasen yo. Bureeki desu yo.
        "That's not the accelerator. It's the brake."

a̒kushon アクション (<action)

Akushon, from English *action,* is quite limited in meaning in that it is generally used only with reference to action in movies, plays, etc., as in

(1) Ano kantoku wa akushon no tsuke-kata ga joozu da to iwarete-iru.
    "They say that director is good at teaching how to perform in specific scenes."
(2) Seibugeki wa futsuu akushon ga ooi.
    "Westerns are usually full of action."

anime アニメ (<*anima*tion)

Anime is an abbreviated version of *a̒nime̒eshon,*

which comes from English *animation.* Unlike the English, however, *anime* (or *animeeshon*) means only one thing, i. e. "the process of preparing animated cartoons, or its product."

anpu アンプ (< *amp*lifier)

Amplifier, meaning "electric component which amplifies sound," is *a˥npurifa˥iaa* in Japanese, or more commonly *anpu* for short. Whether *anpu* is a Japan-made abbreviation or should be traced to the short English form, *amp,* however, is hard to determine.

The non-loan equivalent *de˥npa-zoofuku˥ki* is practically never used in speech.

a˥tora˥kushon アトラクション (< attraction)

Atorakushon has a limited meaning and is used exclusively in the entertainment world to mean "a small bit of extra entertainment added to the main show at a theater to attract more people." Since this is the only meaning of *atorakushon,* one cannot talk about, for example, the *atorakushon* of a beautiful woman, meaning "attractive quality."

a˥uto-da˥iningu アウト・ダイニング (lit. out-dining)

Although not frequently, *auto-dainingu* is used to

mean "dining out" (Jiyūkokuminsha, 1976, p. 1343). This pseudo-loan reflects the word order of its more common non-loan counterpart *gaishoku* 外食, the first character of which means "out," and the second "eating."

a⌈uto-se⌉kkusu   アウト・セックス   (lit. out-sex)

Extramarital sex is called *auto-sekkusu,* a new pseudo-loan. Of all the dictionaries I consulted, Jiyūkokuminsha (1981, p. 857) is the only one that lists this word.

Ba⌈ado-Ui⌉iku   バード・ウイーク   (lit. Bird Week)

The week starting on May 10th was designated as *Baado-Uiiku* "Bird Week" in Japan in 1950, and it has been observed as such since then. The purpose of *Baado-Uiiku* is to promote the protection of wild birds. Although its non-loan equivalent *A⌈ichoo-Shu⌉ukan* 愛鳥週間 is sometimes used, the loanword version, because of its Western flavor, sounds more up-to-date and therefore desirable. Second, it is written in katakana, which makes it easier, especially for youngsters, to read and remember.

baaten   バーテン   (<*barten*der)

A bartender is called a *ba⌈ate⌉ndaa* in Japan. Since it is a long word, it is often shortened to *baaten.* There is no non-loan counterpart. It is my conjecture that, al-

though every bar-goer in Japan is familiar with the word
baaten or *baatendaa* and knows what a *baaten* does, not
many know that the original English word *bartender* is
a combination of *bar* and *tender* and therefore means "a
person who tends to customers' orders at a bar."

(1)   Asoko no baaten wa nakanaka hansamu da nee.
       "The bartender of that bar is pretty handsome,
       isn't he?"

ba⌐iko⌐rojii   バイコロジー   (<bicology)

The word *bicology* first appeared in America about
1970 as a combination of *bike* and *ecology*. It was coined
as a gimmick to urge people to ride bicycles, instead of
driving cars, for the purpose of environmental protection.
The word was introduced to Japan about 1973. Since it
was the time of the first oil crisis, the word really caught
on in Japan. It is ironic that some gimmicky expressions
originally coined in America survive in Japan, sometimes
long after they have fallen into disuse in the United States.

ba⌐ipure⌐eyaa   バイプレーヤー   (lit. byplayer)

A supporting actor or actress is called either *wakiya-
ku,* a non-loan, or *baipureeyaa,* a pseudo-loan. *Baipureeyaa* is such a cleverly made pseudo-loan that most scholars don't seem to realize that there is no such word as
*byplayer in English. Of all the dictionaries and other

publications I consulted, Bunkachō (p. 69) was the only one that pointed this out. In fact, most loanword dictionaries list the nonexistent English **byplayer* as the origin of *baipureeyaa!*

ba⌈kkubo⌉on　バックボーン　(<backbone)

The word for *backbone* is usually *sebone* or *sekitsui.*

(1)　Ano hito wa sebone (*or* sekitsui) ga chotto magatte-iru.

"His backbone (*or* spine) is slightly curved."

The loanword *bakkuboon* (from *backbone*) is used only for the figurative meaning of "strength of character."

(2)　Ano seijika wa bakkuboon ga nakute dame da.

"That politician has no backbone and is therefore not much good."

The non-loan *kikotsu* could be used in this sense, but *bakkuboon* sounds more modern.

ba⌈kku-ho⌉omu　バック・ホーム　(lit. back home)

Bakku-hoomu does not refer to someone being back at his home. It is strictly a baseball term coined in Japan from *ba⌈kku* (<back) plus *ho⌉omu* (<home) to mean "Throw the ball to the plate!", and is most frequently used as a command to a fielder who has just caught the ball.

ba⌐ndo⌐man   バンドマン   (<*bandsman*)

English *bandsman* should have yielded **ba⌐nzu⌐man* in Japanese, but instead it became *bandoman*. The reason for this is fairly easy to explain. Because both *ba⌐ndo* and *ma⌐n* were familiar terms already, their combination was also easily understandable to everyone, whereas *banzuman would have sounded strange and unfamiliar. Another possible factor might be the existence of English compounds (such as *bandmaster*) which contain *band* rather than *bands*. *Bandmaster*, of course, yielded *ba⌐ndo-ma⌐sutaa* in Japanese. From *bandomasutaa*, it was just a short step to *bandoman*.

Ba⌐rentain⌐-Dee   バレンタイン・デー
                        (<*Valentine's Day*)

When *Valentine's Day* became a Japanese word, the possessive ending, *'s*, was dropped, as was the case with some other loanwords such as *ba⌐ttaa-bo⌐kkusu* (<*batter's box*) and *fī⌐rudaa-cho⌐isu* (<*fielder's choice*).

Valentine's Day was not known in Japan until the 1960's, when commercialism picked it up. The way *Barentain-Dee* is observed in Japan, however, is quite different from the practice in the United States. In America, it is a day for exchanging cards and gifts, chiefly between husband and wife or between lovers. In Japan, on the other hand, gift giving on *Barentain-Dee* is one-way traffic from women to men. Women give boxes of candies to men whom they secretly love. It is, as it were, the Japanese version of Sadie Hawkins' Day.

ba῾su バス (<bass)

In addition to *basu* meaning "bus" and *basu* meaning "bath," there is another *basu*, which originates from *bass*, a musical term. This *basu* is based on a misreading of the original English word, *bass*. Although, in English, *bass* is pronounced exactly like *base*, when it was introduced into Japanese, the pronunciation was influenced by the spelling, thus yielding *basu*.

(1)   Ano hito no koe wa sugoi basu da ne.

     "That man's voice is a tremendous bass."

Be῾esu, a version closer to the English pronunciation, is sometimes used also.

ba῾suteru バステル (lit. *bus*+ho*tel*)

Passin (p. 167) claims that he has seen what is advertised as a *basuteru* in Japan. It is, according to him, a kind of motel which caters to people traveling by bus! This is, of course, another pseudo-loan.

ba῾ton-ga῾aru バトン・ガール (lit. baton girl)

What is known as a majorette or a drum majorette in English is a *baton-gaaru* in Japan. Apparently, instead of borrowing *majorette* or *drum majorette* directly into their language, Japanese speakers decided to coin a new compound by combining the already familiar terms *baton* and *gāaru*. *Bāton-towāaraa* (lit. baton twirler) also appears in Yoshizawa (p. 219), but it is probably not as common as *baton-gaaru*.

baˈton-taˈtchi バトン・タッチ (lit. baton touch)

This is a sports term used in track. It is a pseudo-loan created from *baton* "baton" and *taˈtchi* "touch" with the meaning of "the passing of a baton between two members of a relay team."

(1) Baton-tatchi ga heta de makete-shimaimashita.

"We lost because of poor baton passing."

The word is also used figuratively to refer, for example, to the passing of power from one prime minister to the next.

(2) Nihon no shushoo wa tokidoki kawaru ga, baton-tatchi ga itsumo umaku iku to wa kagiranai.

"In Japan, the prime minister is replaced from time to time, and the transition does not always go smoothly."

baundo バウンド (<bound)

When a ball bounces, it is a *baundo* in Japanese, which is presumably derived from English *bound*. Although it is true that one of the meanings of *bound* given in the English dictionary is "bounce", in American baseball, for example, no one speaks of the ball "bounding." The ball "bounces" instead. In Japan, on the other hand, it is always *baundo*. *Bounce* somehow has not found its way into Japanese as yet.

A bad hop is *i¯regyuraa-ba¯undo* (lit. irregular bound).

(1) Booru wa hoomu-pureeto no mae de ookiku baundo-shite, kyatchaa no atama o koshimashita.

"The ball took a big bounce in front of the home plate and went over the catcher."

be¯bii-gya¯ngu ベビー・ギャング (lit. baby gang)

Bebii-gyangu probably originates from the title of the cartoon with the same name that was popular in the '50s. The cartoon's main character was a little boy who was as mischievous as Dennis the Menace. He always wore a black mask over his eyes and carried a toy gun. Hence the name *bebiigyangu*, meaning "baby gangster." The word thus came to mean "mischievous child that causes everyone big headaches."

be¯bii-ho¯teru ベビー・ホテル (lit. baby hotel)

Bebii-hoteru refers to 24-hour commercial baby-sitting agencies for very young babies. They were, at least at one point in the past, poorly equipped and did not even have well-qualified employees trained to take care of little babies. They became notorious about 1980 or 81 after a few babies died from sheer neglect at some *bebii-hoteru.*

A *bebii-hoteru* is different from a *hoikujo,* a government-run daycare center.

be⌐bii-sa⌐akuru   ベビー・サークル   (lit. baby circle)

In Japan, a playpen is known as *bebii-saakuru,* a pseudo-loan.
(1)   Uchi no ko wa itsumo bebii-saakuru ni irete asoba-sete-okimasu.

"I always let my child play in the playpen."

My guess is that *bebii-saakuru* are not as popular in Japan as playpens are in the United States. At least two reasons readily come to mind. First, since Japanese rooms are small, a *bebii-saakuru* would really become a big obstacle for the rest of the family. Second, to most Japanese, the idea of keeping a little child pent-up in a *bebii-saakuru* would be like treating him like an animal. They would rather let their little child crawl around freely even if that might lead to trouble.

be⌐bii-suto⌐ppu   ベビー・ストップ   (lit. baby stop)

This is a pseudo-loan coined by putting two already familiar loans together. It is a slang expression meaning "abortion." The technical term for *abortion* is a non-loan, *ni⌐nshin-chu⌐uzetsu,* which literally means "pregnancy stoppage." The word formation for *bebii-sutoppu* seems to have followed the same pattern.

be⌐ddo⌐-in ベッド・イン (lit. bed in)

Beddo-in means "[lovers] going to bed together." It is very interesting that *beddo-in* follows the same word order as *be⌐ddo ni hairu* "to go into bed." There are other pseudo-loans that follow the same pattern, e.g. *go⌐oru⌐-in* (lit. goal in) meaning "reaching the goal" and *kya⌐npu⌐-in* (lit. camp in) meaning "starting training camp."

(1) Ano futa-ri wa zuibun naka ga yokatta ga beddo-in made wa ikanakatta rashii.

"Those two were very close, but it seems that they did not go as far as going to bed together."

be⌐niya-i⌐ta ベニヤ板 (<veneer+Japanese *ita* "board")

Veneer was introduced into Japanese in the Taisho era (1912-26) and became *beniya* (Arakawa, p. 1207). Later, however, the non-loan word *i⌐ta* "board" was added to form *beniya-ita* (lit. veneer board). *Veneer board* would, of course, be redundant in English, but since *beniya* alone would have sounded a little too unfamiliar to most Japanese, it is quite understandable why *ita* was added to make the meaning clear. Concerning this point,

Umegaki (1975b, p. 208) proposes an extremely interesting hypothesis. He suggests that *beniya* must have been misinterpreted by some Japanese as the name of a lumber dealer since, as everyone knows, the names of many Japanese stores, dealers, and manufacturers have the suffix *-ya* at the end, as in the case of Matsu-ya and Fuji-ya. According to Umegaki, people who thus analyzed the word as *Beni* plus *-ya* must have added *ita* to indicate "boards manufactured by Beni-ya"! Be that as it may, *beniya-ita* has since then come to mean not only "veneer" but also "plywood." In other words, although *veneer* and *plywood* mean two different things in English, *beniya-ita* covers the meanings of both in Japanese.

bɪggu   ビッグ (<big)

The Japanese word for *big* is normally o͡okiĩ, as in
(1)   Tookyoo wa Oosaka yori *ookii.*
      "Tokyo is bigger than Osaka."

The loanword *biggu,* from English *big,* is not used alone but only in certain compounds such as *bi͡ggu-ge͡emu* "a big game," *bi͡ggu-ebe͡nto* "a big event," and *bi͡ggu-nyu͡usu* "big news."
(2)   Senkyuuhyakuhachijuu-nen no biggu-nyuusu wa
      daitooryoo-senkyo de Reegan ga katta koto datta.
      "The big news of 1980 was Reagan's victory in the presidential election."

bi⌐jinesu-ho⌐teru　ビジネス・ホテル

(lit. business hotel)

Bijinesu-hoteru is a pseudo-loan meaning "hotel for businessmen." A *bijinesu-hoteru* as a rule does not cater to tourists. It is not a luxurious hotel like the New Otani or the Imperial. It is usually located near a main railroad station, and its rates are reasonable. A typical *bijinesu-hoteru* in Tokyo would be Dai-ichi near Shinbashi Station.

bi⌐suta-ka⌐a　ビスタ・カー　(lit. vista car)

An observation car is usually called *te⌐nboo⌐-sha,* a non-loan. In 1958, however, Kinki Railways started operating a two-level observation car (Yoshizawa, p. 35), and called it *bisuta-kaa* instead of *tenboo-sha,* obviously to make it sound like something really innovative. *Observation car,* if adopted verbatim, would have yielded **o⌐buzabeeshon-ka⌐a,* which would have been much too long. That was probably why the simpler *bista-kaa* was coined by translating *tenboo-sha* (*tenboo* "vista" plus *sha* "car") directly into English.

bo⌐oi-suka⌐uto　ボーイ・スカウト　(<*Boy Scout*s)

In Japanese, *booi-sukauto* (lit. boy scout) means "Boy Scouts." In other words, it refers to the organization of Boy Scouts and not to an individual member. Individual members are *booi-sukauto no dan'in* (lit. member[s] of Boy Scouts).

Ga⌐aru-suka⌐uto (lit. girl scout) functions the same way in that it refers only to the organization of Girl Scouts and not to a member thereof.

buraindo   ブラインド   (<blind)

English *blind* in the sense of "window shade" is *buraindo* in Japanese. There is no non-loan equivalent.

(1)   Hi ga mabushii deshoo. Buraindo o oroshimashoo ka.

"Isn't the sun too bright for you?   Shall I pull down the shade?"

She⌐edo, from English *shade,* on the other hand, usually means either "awning" (Yoshizawa, p. 188) or "lamp shade."

(2)   Ano uchi de wa mado no soto-gawa ni zenbu sheedo o tsuketeiru.

"That house has an awning outside every window."

(3)   Kono sutando no sheedo wa Mitsukoshi de kaimashita.

"I bought the shade for this desk lamp at Mitsukoshi."

Sheedo in sentence (2) above may be replaced by the non-loan *hiyoke,* whereas *sheedo* in sentence (3) is the equivalent of *ka⌐sa,* a non-loan.

bu⌐re¬eki ブレーキ (<brake)

    Bureeki means "brake." Usually English words end-
ing with a *k* yield loanwords ending with *ku* (not *ki*),
e.g. *no⌐kku* "knock" and *mi⌐ruku* "milk." Some English
words, however, as is the case with *bu⌐re¬eki* and *ke⌐eki*
"cake," have yielded loanwords ending with *ki.* Ichikawa
(p. 199) explains thus: "...we at once recognize that
the parasitic vowel *i* was added where the neighboring
vowel was a front vowel like *e* and *i*...."

(1)   Bureeki no kikanai kuruma wa abunai.

     "A car that doesn't brake well is a hazard."

bu⌐ro¬okun ブロークン (<broken)

    Burookun has only one specialized meaning: "im-
perfectly spoken." Of the following examples, therefore,
(1) is correct, but (2) is not.

(1)   Ano hito no eigo wa burookun de, sappari waka-
     ranai.

     "His English is so broken I can hardly understand
     it."

(2)   *Kono chawan wa burookun da.

     "This cup is broken."

To express the intended meaning in (2), one would have
to use the non-loan *ko⌐wa¬rete-iru* "broken," as in

(3)   Kono chawan wa kowarete-iru.

buˈruˈu-dee ブルー・デー (lit. blue day)

Buruu-dee is a euphemism for *seˈiriˈ-bi* (lit. menstruation day). It is a pseudo-loan coined probably by someone who knew that in English *blue* meant "depressed."

chaˈko チャコ (<chalk)

Chako, from English *chalk,* refers to a special kind of chalk used for marking in sewing. The regular kind of chalk used for writing on a blackboard is *choˈoku,* also from *chalk.* The fact that *chako* does not reflect the spelling of *chalk* indicates that the word was learned through the ear.

Chalk is one of the limited number of English words that have yielded more than one corresponding loanword in Japanese. Other examples of this type are *iron* (which has become both *aian* "an iron-headed golf club" and *airon* "an iron for pressing clothes") and *ruby* (which has produced both *ruˈbi* "small *kana* printed alongside Chinese characters" and *ruˈbii* "a kind of jewel").

channeru チャンネル (<channel)

This word came into Japan together with television. It is therefore used only as a television term meaning "television channel." One speaks of, for example, *Daˈi-Yon Chaˈnneru* "Channel 4" and *Daˈi-Roku Chaˈnneru* "Channel 6."

(1) Sonna ni channeru o kirikaete bakari iru to, daiaru
ga kowarete-shimaimasu yo.
"If you keep switching channels like that, you'll
end up ruining the dial."

che⌐nji-re⌐baa チェンジ・レバー   (lit. change lever)

A gearshift is known as *chenji-rebaa* in Japanese—
one of the many pseudo-loans referring to parts of a
car. Other examples are *handoru* (lit. handle) "steering
wheel" and *ba⌐kku-mi⌐raa* (lit. back mirror) "rear-view
mirror."

chi⌐kin-ra⌐isu チキン・ライス   (lit. chicken rice)

After Western cooking was introduced into Japan
during the Meiji era, the Japanese invented some semi-
Western dishes that are still very popular today, e.g.
ka⌐ree-ra⌐isu (lit. curry rice, i.e. curry served with rice),
ton-katsu "[Japanese-style] pork cutlet," and *ko⌐rokke*
"croquette." *Chikin-raisu* is another of those semi-West-
ern dishes. It is fried rice mixed with little bits of
chicken, onion, and green peas, and seasoned with
tomato ketchup.

chi⌐kku チック   (<cosme*tic*?)

Chikku refers to a stick of scented vaselin for men's

hair. Although the origin of the word is obscure, most scholars seem to believe that it was originated from the final portion of *cosmetic,* e.g. Umegaki (1975b, p. 200), Arakawa (p. 747), and Yoshizawa (p. 131). Umegaki claims that it was quite common in early Meiji to truncate long loanwords, e.g. *furanneru* shortened to *ne⌐ru.* I would like to venture a new conjecture here, however. It seems to me that *chikku* may very well have come from English *stick.*

chokki   チョッキ   (<jack?)

The etymology of *chokki* meaning "vest" has not been clearly determined. Umegaki (1975b, pp. 175-76) even cites, in fun, a folk etymology which associated the word with Japanese "*chot*to *ki*ru," meaning "to put on something light." Scholars are divided in tracing *chokki* to English *jacket* (Ueda & Matsui), French *jaque* (Nihon Kokugo Dai-jiten), Portuguese *jaque* (Yoshizawa, p. 81), and English *jack* (Kōjien, p. 1463). Umegaki suggests (ibid.) that Dutch *jack* is just as good a possibility as any other alternative. It is my conjecture that toward the end of the Edo Period, either English *jack,* Dutch *jack,* or French *jaque* was introduced into Japanese as a military term meaning "sleeveless jacket worn by foot soldiers," and later came to mean "vest [worn by civilians]" after going through phonetic transformation.

(1)   Uwagi, chokki, zubon de mitsu-zoroi ni naru.

"A jacket, a vest, and trousers form a three-piece suit."

da⌐asu ダース (<dozen)

Daasu, from English *dozen,* came into Japanese during the Meiji era. As was the case with early loans, this one too may have been learned entirely aurally. Hence the dropping of the final *n* sound. On the other hand, the dropping of the *n* sound may have been due to the written form *doz.* (i. e. a shorter, abbreviated version of *dozen* or *dozens*), which some Japanese are likely to have misinterpreted as a complete word.

(1) Enpitsu wa Nihon de mo *daasu* de utte-imasu.

"Pencils are sold by the *dozen* in Japan also."

de⌐ddo-bo⌐oru デッド・ボール (lit. dead ball)

In Japanese baseball, *deddo-booru* (from English *dead ball*) is misused to mean "hit batsman." This misapplication probably stems from the fact that, when a pitch hits a batter, the ball is considered "dead," i.e. "out of play."

(1) Oh-senshu deddo-booru de ichi-rui ni demashita.

"Oh goes to first, hit by a pitch."

de⌈ddo-hi⌉ito デッド・ヒート (<dead heat)

Deddo-hiito is a sports term. At first sight, it looks as though it is used in the same way as the original English term, *dead heat.* But on closer examination, one must agree with Hani (p. 77) that *deddo-hiito* is another example of a misapplied loanword. In English, *dead heat* has something to do with how a race ends, for it means "a race in which two or more competitors finish in a tie," as in *A and B finished in a virtual dead heat.* In Japanese, on the other hand, *deddo-hiito* has something to do with how a race runs, and not necessarily with how a race ends, for it means "a very close contest." Hani cites the following sentence as an illustration:

(1) Deddo-hiito o enjita sue, naniboo ga katta.

Literally the sentence means "After a dead heat, so-and-so won." A more precise English version, however, should be "After a close race, so-and-so won."

de⌈za⌉inaa デザイナー (<designer)

Most commonly *dezainaa* means "dress designer." Lately, however, the word has expanded its range of meaning to include commercial designers and industrial designers as well.

(1) Furansu no dezainaa wa Nihon de mo yuumei desu.

   "French designers are famous in Japan also."

di͞suko ディスコ (<disco)

English *discotheque* and *disco* have been introduced into Japanese to become *di͞sukote͞eku* "discotheque" and *disuko* "disco," respectively. Other disco-related compounds have also become popular such as *di͞suko-da͞nsu* "disco dance," *di͞suko-myu͞ujikku* "disco music," *di͞suko-sa͞undo* "disco sound," *di͞suko-do͞resu,* and *di͞suko-fa͞s-shon* (Fukao, pp. 70-71).

Disuko, as explained above, comes directly from English *disco*. In other words, it is not a Japan-made abbreviation, as some people mistakenly claim (see Yoshizawa & Ishiwata, p. 348).

(1) Konban wa disuko e itte odorimashoo.

"Let's go to a disco and dance tonight."

do͞a-a͞i ドア・アイ (lit. door eye)

A peephole through which one sees who is outside the door is a *doa-ai* in Japanese.

(1) Genkan no doa ni doa-ai o tsuketa hoo ga anzen deshoo.

"It will be safer to have a peephole installed in your front door."

do͞a-suto͞ppaa ドア・ストッパー (lit. door stopper)

A rubber-tipped projection for preventing a door from striking a wall is a *doa-sutoppaa*. The word must have been coined by a Japanese with a considerable knowledge of English, who, upon coming across the English word *doorstop,* must have felt it needed the suffix *-er* to make it an agent noun. Hence *doa-sutoppaa* instead of ** doa-sutoppu.*

do⌐kutaa-suto⌐ppu   ドクター・ストップ

(lit. doctor stop)

Dokutaa-sutoppu seems to follow the same word-formation pattern as other *-sutoppu* words such as *en*[jin]*-suto*[ppu] (lit. *engine stop,* meaning "the stopping of a car engine") and *be⌐bii-suto⌐ppu* (lit. baby stop, meaning "the stopping of the coming of a baby," i.e. "abortion"), but it actually does not. *Dokutaa-sutoppu* does not mean "the stopping of a doctor," but rather "*doctor-stop*ped contest," particularly "boxing match stopped by the ring doctor."

By extension, this word may be applied to other situations also. For example, if you have to give up smoking on your doctor's advice, you might jokingly refer to it as *dokutaa-sutoppu* (Passin, p. 167).

(1)   A: Tabako o oyame ni natta n desu ka.
           "Have you stopped smoking?"
      B: Dokutaa-sutoppu na n desu yo.
           "I was told to by my doctor."

do¬n-mai ドン・マイ (lit. *Don't mi*nd!)

Never mind, meaning "It's of no concern," came into Japanese and became *don-mai.* It is used only in such sports as baseball and volleyball as a word of encouragement for a teammate who has just committed an error, and it is usually repeated once, as in

(1)   Don-mai, don-mai!

   "Don't worry [about your error]!"

Ne⌐baa-ma⌐in, directly from *never mind,* is also used sometimes (Yoshizawa, p. 292), but, in my view, not even half as often as *don-mai.*

do⌐ra¬ibaa ドライバー (<screw*driver*)

A screwdriver used to be called a *ne⌐jima⌐washi,* a non-loan. Recently, however, *doraibaa* (from *screwdriver*) has become more and more popular. According to Nishio (p. 178), with the exception of the old generation, the Japanese much prefer *doraibaa* to *nejimawashi*; junior high school students, for example, use *doraibaa* almost five times as often as *nejimawashi.*

The full form, *su⌐kuryuudora⌐ibaa,* is apparently rarely used except when referring to a kind of cocktail, i.e. a drink made with vodka mixed with orange juice.

do⌐raibu-ma¬ppu ドライブ・マップ (lit. drive map)

Doraibu-mappu is a pseudo-loan coined from *do⌐ra⌐ibu*

"drive" and *mappu* "map" to mean "road map." The
reason this new word was created instead of directly
borrowing *road map* must have been that *roodo-mappu
would not have implied driving in Japanese.

(1)   Hakone made no doraibu-mappu ga attara kashite-
       kudasai.
       "If you have a road map to Hakone, please lend it
       to me."

do⌐rai-mi⌐ruku   ドライ・ミルク   (<dry milk)

Dorai-miruku meaning "dry milk" is probably not
used as often as *hunnyuu* (a non-loan) or *ko⌐na-mi⌐ruku*
(Japanese *ko⌐na⌐* "powder"+loanword *mi⌐ruku* "milk"),
both meaning "powdered milk."

In Japan, some scholars (e.g. Ishiwata, p. 144) seem
to believe that *dorai-miruku* comes from *dried milk,* the
-ed ending of which must have been dropped in the
process of borrowing. What they don't realize is that, in
English, *dry milk* is just as correct as *dried milk,* and
that *dorai-miruku* therefore may just as well be derived
from *dry milk.* This is a different case from such loanwords as *ko⌐ndensu-mi⌐ruku* (lit. condense milk). In the
latter case, it is clear that the past participle ending, *-ed,*
was indeed dropped in Japanese, for *condensed milk,*
not **condense milk,* is the only correct English term.

do⌐ron-ge⌐emu ドロン・ゲーム （＜drawn game)

Doron-geemu, meaning "tie game," is strictly a base-ball term. It is probably not as common as the non-loan *hikiwake* "tie" or the newer loan *ta⌐i-ge⌐emu* (＜tie game), but it is still used once in a while by old base-ball fans perhaps.

DPE (＜*d*evelopment, *p*rinting, *e*nlarging)

Japanese camera shops and photo-processing shops often have large DPE signs in the front. Japanese tour-ists in the United States may look for similar signs in vain, for this particular abbreviation is, of course, never used in America. Apparently, this ingenious invention is ascribable to some enterprising camera store owner in Japan. DPE not only is much simpler to read or write but stands out far more than its non-loan equivalent, 現像・焼付・引伸, *genzoo-yakitsuke-hikinobashi.*

e⌐ba-mi⌐ruku エバ・ミルク （＜*eva*porated *milk*)

Eba-miruku or *e⌐baa-mi⌐ruku* is an abbreviation of *e⌐baporeeteddo-mi⌐ruku,* which refers to thick, unsweeten-ed, canned milk. The shorter form is preferred because the full form is much too long for most Japanese. The non-loan equivalent, *mu⌐too-re⌐nnyuu,* is probably used only as a written form.

e⌐be⌐nto エベント (＜event)

Ebento or *i⌐be⌐nto* is rarely used by itself. It appears mainly as part of such compounds as *bi⌐ggu-ebe⌐nto* "big event" and *me⌐en-ebe⌐nto* "main event." These two compounds almost exclusively refer to sports events.

(1) Kyoo no meen-ebento wa mochiron Ari to Hoomu-zu no shiai da.

   "Today's main event is, of course, the match between Ali and Holmes."

e⌐chike⌐tto エチケット (＜etiquette)

Echiketto is used more or less interchangeably with the non-loan *re⌐igi-sa⌐hoo,* but since it comes from English, it sounds more modern than the non-loan counterpart.

(1) Anna echiketto o shiranai hito to tsukiai-takunai.

   "I don't want to associate with someone like that who lacks etiquette."

Echiketto was highlighted in the early '60s, when the then Premier Hayato Ikeda publicly mispronounced it *ekechitto.* Most people interpreted it as a sign of ignorance and had a hearty laugh although it may have been just a slip of the tongue.

e⌐eru エール (＜yell)

Just before an intercollegiate baseball game, there is

often a brief ceremony called ee̅ru no kookan, meaning "exchange of eeru." This eeru is purported to have come from English yell. Whereas, in English, yelling is not limited to specific utterances or occasions, Japanese eeru has only one narrow meaning: "the act of yelling out in unison a specified set of words in order to cheer for one's athletic, particularly baseball, team." In the case of Tokyo University, at least while I was a student there, the words used to be *Huree, huree, Toodai!* (lit. Hurray, hurray, Tokyo University!), which was uttered rather slowly by the cheerleaders once and repeated quickly by the other students twice in a row. It is my conjecture that this format has not changed much since then.

e̅esu エース (<ace)

Many of the meanings of the original English word, *ace*, were transferred to Japanese *eesu*: (1) a playing card with a single spot (although *ichi* "one" is also used), (2) a service ace in tennis, volleyball, etc. (also known as sa̅abisu-e̅esu "service ace"), (3) a hole in one (in golf), and (4) the most reliable member of an athletic team, especially the best pitcher on a baseball team (although, in English, *ace pitcher* is probably the norm rather than *ace* by itself).

(1) Tookyoo Jaiantsu no eesu wa Egawa desu ka.

"Is the ace pitcher for the Tokyo Giants Egawa?"

Eesu, however, does not carry some other meanings

of *ace,* e. g. "a fighter pilot who has shot down more than five enemy craft."

e⌐konomikku-a⌐nimaru エコノミック・アニマル
(＜economic animal)

The expression *ekonomikku-animaru* is traced to the late Zulfiqar Ali Bhutto, who, as Foreign Minister of Pakistan, referred to the Japanese as "economic animals" in June, 1965, in criticism of their ruthless economic invasion of South and South-East Asia (Yoshizawa and Ishiwata, p. 86). Although he was executed as traitor in the late '70s by his own countrymen, his coinage has remained in Japanese as *ekonomikku-animaru.* Even today, the Japanese use the word as a warning to themselves against overzealousness in economic activities, especially in trading with foreign countries.

(1)   Wareware wa ekonomikku-animaru to yobarenai
        yoo ni shinakerebanaranai.
        "We must try not to be called 'economic animals.' "

e⌐naaji⌐suto エナージスト (lit. energy＋ist)

I don't believe this pseudo-loan is widely used since only one of the many reference works I consulted lists it. According to Ishiwata (p. 140), *enaajisuto* was coined in Japan from *energy* and *-ist* to mean "energetic person."

e⌐ndo⌐-ran　エンド・ラン　(<hit-*and-run*)

Endo-ran is a shorter version of *hi⌐tto-endo-ra⌐n* "hit-and-run play." It is strictly a baseball term referring to a play in which the base runner starts running to the next base as the pitcher delivers a pitch to the batter, who must then hit the ball.

There was once a time when the full form, *hitto-endo-ran,* was the norm, but since the word was a little too long, someone started shortening it to *endo-ran,* which has since then become more popular than the full form. Some people even say *ra⌐n-endo-hi⌐tto* (lit. run-and-hit) according to Hani (p. 36), but that is an entirely Japanese coinage which has no English counterpart.

Whereas, in Japanese, *endo-ran* is a noun, English *hit-and-run* is an adjective. The equivalent of *endo-ran* in English would therefore be not *hit-and-run* but *hit-and-run play.*

(1)　Endo-ran ga seikoo-shite, ichi-rui no rannaa san-rui ni tasshimashita.

　　"They pull a hit-and-run play, and the first-base runner reaches third."

e⌐ngeeji-ri⌐ngu　エンゲージ・リング

(<*engage*ment *ring*)

Engeeji-ringu comes from *engagement ring.* The fact that the full form, *e⌐ngeejimento-ri⌐ngu,* is not listed in most dictionaries, except perhaps Arakawa (p. 178), shows that the shorter form is the norm. There is a non-loan equivalent, *ko⌐n'yaku-yu⌐biwa,* but it sounds old-fashioned.

(1) Takahashi-san wa engeeji-ringu o hamete-iru kara,
    moo sugu kekkon-suru n deshoo.
    "Miss Takahashi's wearing an engagement ring. I
    suppose she'll be getting married pretty soon."

e⌐njin-ki⌐i   エンジン・キー   (lit. engine key)

An ignition key for an automobile is usually called *enjin-kii,* which was obviously coined by combining two already familiar loans, *e⌐njin* "engine" and *ki⌐i* "key." *I⌐gunisshon-ki⌐i* "ignition key" is also used, but probably not as commonly as *enjin-kii.* After all, *enjin-kii* not only sounds more familiar to most Japanese, but it also is shorter.

e⌐nko   えんこ

Passin (p. 165) speculates that just as *en-suto* (see *en-suto*) is derived from "*eng*ine+*sto*p," *enko* must come from *engine* plus Japanese *koshoo* "breakdown." Although this is an extremely interesting theory, I must call it a misconception. It is actually not even a partial loan. It is instead traceable to an expression used in baby talk meaning "to sit" or "to squat." By extension, it is used to refer to a vehicle stranded on the road.

(1) Basu ga enko-shite-shimatta n desu.
"The bus I was on broke down."

e⌐reki-gi⌐taa エレキ・ギター (<*electric guitar*)

Electricity is called *de⌐nki,* a non-loan, but it used to be called *e⌐reki,* an abbreviation of *e⌐reki⌐toru, e⌐reki⌐teru,* or *e⌐rekiterishite⌐eto,* all of which were derived in the 18th century from Dutch *electriciteit* (Arakawa, pp. 172-73). In due course, *ereki* was gradually replaced by *denki,* which has become the only form currently in use. For some reason, however, when the electric guitar was introduced to Japan in the mid '60s by rock groups such as the Benchers and the Astronauts, *ereki* was revived and became part of the new compound *ereki-gitaa* (Yoshizawa and Ishiwata, p. 93). *Ereki-gitaa* is sometimes shortened to *ereki.*

(1) Tonari no ereki-gitaa ga yakamashikute nemurenai.
"The electric guitar next door is so loud I can't fall asleep."

e⌐ro-guro-na⌐nsensu エロ・グロ・ナンセンス
(lit. *ero*tic, *gro*tesque *nonsense*)

Beginning about 1927, there was a very decadent climate in Japan, which peaked in 1930-31. Cafés and bars featured lewdness, theaters offered racy shows, and literature too turned erotic, grotesque, and nonsensical.

This period is sometimes referred to as *e⌐ro-guro-nansensu-ji⌐dai* (lit. era of erotic, grotesque nonsense).

e⌐suke⌐epu エスケープ (<escape)

In addition to being a wrestling term meaning "the act of slipping out of the opponent's hold to score a point," *esukeepu* is also used by students to refer to the act of slipping out of class or school, especially in the verb form *e⌐suke⌐epu-suru* "to escape," as in

(1) Ano sensei no jugyoo wa tsumaranai kara, kyoo mo tochuu de esukeepu-shiyoo.

   "That teacher's class is so boring. Let's slip away again today before it's over."

In this latter sense, *esukeepu-suru* may seem synonymous with *sa⌐bo⌐-ru* meaning "to play hooky," but they are not the same. Committing *esukeepu* is, in a way, more thrilling than *sabo-ru* because it requires more skill on the part of the student, who has to slip out of class unnoticed, while the teacher is busy writing on the blackboard. Also, *esukeepu* is strictly student lingo whereas *sabo-ru* is more widely used. For example, one may say *ka⌐isha o sabo⌐-ru* "to be unjustifiably absent from work (lit. from one's company)," but not **ka⌐isha o eske⌐epu-suru*.

fa⌐kku ファック (<f---)

Fakku from the famed four-letter English word *f---*

came into use probably in the late '60s or the early '70s. I remember the shock I experienced some years ago when I found *fakku* repeatedly used in an article by a well-known writer published in *The Asahi,* which is considered the most prestigious newspaper in Japan. Can anyone imagine the English word *f---* printed in, say, *The New York Times*?

Passin (p. 118) reports seeing a huge streamer hanging down the front of a midtown Tokyo movie theater with a large inscription "Fa⌈kku-E⌉iga (lit. f--- movie, i.e. movie with many f---ing scenes)!" His interpretation (p. 119) is that *fakku,* being a loan, probably is accepted as more indirect and less strident than non-loans referring to sexual intercourse, and that *fakku-eiga* must sound more modern and respectable (!) than other loans or semi-loans such as *e⌈ro-e⌉iga* "erotic movies" and *bu⌈ruu-fi⌉rumu* "blue film."

Japanese people who come into contact with English speakers, however, must realize that the original English word is, to say the least, far more strident than its Japanese derivative, and they therefore ought to refrain from using it in English at any cost.

fa⌈ntaji⌉kku ファンタジック (<*fantastic*)

Although *fantajikku* is ascribed to English *fantastic* in loanword dictionaries such as Arakawa (p. 1075) and Sanseidō (p. 574), my conjecture (although I cannot produce any concrete evidence to support my claim) is that it was created in Japan from *Fa⌐nta⌐jia,* the Japanese title of the Disney movie *Fantasia.* This hypothesis could explain the use of *ji* in *fantajikku.* If the word is indeed derived from *fantastic,* why *ji*?

Moreover, the meaning of *fantajikku* is much more reminiscent of the movie *Fantasia* than of the English word *fantastic. Fantajikku* usually means "dreamlike" in Japanese. Whatever creates an atmosphere of dreamlike fantasy, as did the movie *Fantasia,* is *fantajikku,* as in *fa⌐ntaji⌐kku na fun'iki* "atmosphere" / *supotto-raito* "spot light" / *sakuhin* "opus," etc.

Fantajikku is synonymous with the non-loan *gensoo-teki* but sounds more modern than the latter.

fa⌐unde⌐eshon   ファウンデーション   (<foundation)

The Japanese word for *foundation* is usually *dodai* or *ki⌐so,* as in
(1)   Kono tatemono wa dodai ga shikkari-shite-iru.
      "This building has a solid foundation."
(2)   Kiso ga dekite-ireba, kitto hayaku joozu ni naru deshoo.
      "If you have a good foundation, you will improve quickly, I'm sure."

Faundeeshon, from English *foundation,* is quite specialized in meaning and is most frequently used either to mean "foundation garment" or as an abbreviation of *fa͡undeeshon-kuri͡imu* (<foundation cream) to mean "a cream used as a base for facial make-up."

Faundeeshon in the sense of "foundation cream" is sometimes shortened to *fa͡ndeeshon* or simply *fa͡nde*. This omission of *u* is parallel to the case of *gurando,* which ·is often used instead of *guraundo* (lit. ground, i.e. athletic field).

fe͡a   フェア   (<fair)

Fea has about three meanings in Japanese. First, *fea* refers to a kind of market or exhibition. This use, however, is probably purely commercial and has not yet become very common.

Second, *fea* means "free from dishonesty or injustice," but it is used in this sense by intellectuals only.
(1)   Fea ni tatakatte maketa no da kara, kui wa nai.

"Because I lost a fair fight, I have no regrets."

Third, in baseball, *fea* is the opposite of *fauru* "foul."
(2)   Ima no wa fea datta ka fauru datta ka wakarimasen deshita.

"I couldn't tell whether that one was fair or foul."
Even little children are probably familiar with this last usage.

fe⌐mini⌐suto フェミニスト (<feminist)

Although *feminisuto* obviously comes from English *feminist,* its meaning is quite different from that of the original word. The Japanese version simply means "man who is indulgent with women." For example, a man who gives his seat to a woman, opens a door for a female companion, or frequently brings home a present for his wife is a *feminisuto.* Since Japan is still a male-dominated country, the word *feminisuto* is usually uttered with a ring of sarcasm, as in

(1) Tanaka-san ga mata okusan ni purezento katte-iru
     yo. Ano hito feminisuto da nee.

     "Mr. Tanaka is buying something for his wife again.
     Isn't he a doting husband!"

There is no non-loan equivalent for *feminisuto.* One would have to use a group of words such as *o⌐nna⌐ ni amai otoko* "a man who is indulgent with women."

In English, *feminist* means "person who advocates women's rights." Feminists, therefore, are usually women although there are of course male feminists also. Japanese speakers who mistakenly believe that English *feminist* and Japanese *feminisuto* must refer to the same thing are invariably surprised to find in English-language publications such women as Betty Friedan and Gloria Steinem described as feminists. In Japanese, a real feminist is called by a non-loan, *jo⌐kenkakuchooro⌐nsha,* lit. "a person who advocates expanding women's rights."

fīibaa フィーバー （＜fever）

Fever is normally *ne⌐tsu⌐,* as in

(1) Hidoi kaze o hiite netsu ga aru n desu.

"I have a bad cold with a fever."

Fiibaa is a recent loan which was imported into Japan together with the John Travolta movie "Saturday Night Fever." The word is therefore limited in meaning to signify "intense excitement." For a while after the first showing of the movie in Japan (1977), the new verb *fīibaa-suru* was widely used, especially by weekly magazines. Anyone doing something with great ferver was described as *fiibaa-shite-iru* "doing something with a fever."

fītto-suru フィットする

（＜fit＋Japanese *suru* "to do"）

The English verb *fit* has become a compound verb in Japanese with the addition of *suru* "to do." *Fitto-suru,* however, is used almost exclusively in the area of dressmaking and tailoring, as in

(1) Kono zubon wa uesuto ga yoku fitto-shite-imasu.

"These trousers fit your waist perfectly."

This verb is mostly used by dressmakers and tailors as part of their occupational jargon. Others would probably use non-loans such as *pittari au* "to fit closely."

(2) Kono uwagi ga pittari au kara, kore ni shimasu.

"I'll take this jacket because it fits me just right."

fu⌐raido-po⌐teto   フライド・ポテト   (<fried potato)

Fried potatoes are called *furaido-poteto* (lit. fried potato) or sometimes *po⌐teto-fu⌐rai* (lit. potato fry). As is the case with Japanese nouns, there is no plural form. *Furaido-poteto* refers to all kinds of fried potatoes including french fries. **Fu⌐renchi-fu⌐rai* is never used probably because it does not conjure up an image of potatoes in the minds of most Japanese.

fu⌐raingu-suta⌐ato   フライング・スタート
(<flying start)

Flying start has become *furaingu-sutaato* in Japanese. It is correctly used in auto racing to mean "a start in which the entrants begin moving before reaching the starting line." In other sports such as track and swimming, however, it has long been misused in the sense of "false start." In the latter sense, *furaingu-sutaato* is often shortened to *furaingu*.

(1)   Moo ichi-do furaingu o suru to shikkaku desu.
"He'll be disqualified if he makes another false start."

fu⌐rankufuruto-soose⌐eji   フランクフルト・ソーセージ
(lit. frankfurt sausage)

In English, one might say *frankfurt, frankfurter, frankfort, frankforter,* or simply *frank,* but never **frank-*

furt sausage. Since everyone knows that a frankfurter is a sausage, it would be redundant to attach the word *sausage.* In Japanese, however, *fu⌐rankufu⌐ruto* by itself just sounds like a foreign place name and does not convey the idea of food. Hence *furankufuruto-sooseeji.* In America, a frankfurter is often called a hot dog, but, in Japanese, *ho⌐tto-do⌐ggu* is not interchangeable with *furanku-furuto-sooseeji* (see *hotto-doggu*).

furanneru フランネル (<flannel)

From *flannel* come both *furanneru* and *fu⌐rano.* *Furanneru* was obviously derived from the spelling of the original word whereas *furano* is based on the sound of the word. *Furanneru* (or *ne⌐ru* for short) and *furano* have mutually exclusive functions. *Furanneru* (or *neru*) is mostly for undergarments and pajamas, while *furano* is for Western-style outer garments such as suits and slacks.

(1) furanneru/neru no pajama
    "flannel pajamas"
(2) furano no surakkusu
    "flannel slacks"

fu⌐rii-sa⌐izu フリー・サイズ (lit. free size)

"One size fits all" types of clothing such as socks, stockings, and belts are called *furii-saizu,* a pseudo-loan.
(1) furii-saizu no sutokkingu
    "stockings that fit all sizes"

fuˈroa-sutaˈndo フロア・スタンド (lit. floor stand)

A desk lamp is regularly called a *sutando* in Japanese probably because it "stands" on a desk. By extension, a floor lamp has become a *furoa-sutando* rather than *fuˈ-roa-raˈnpu. The reason *furoa-ranpu is not used, I suppose, is that *raˈnpu* in Japanese is short for *seˈkiyu-raˈnpu* "oil lamp," and does not refer to an electric lamp.

fuˈroˈkku フロック (<fluke)

In sports such as baseball, an accidental win is sometimes called a *furokku* although the word is probably not used as often as the non-loan equivalent, *maguregachi* "accidental victory."

(1) Jaiantsu ni san-do tsuzukete kateba, furokku to wa ienai.

"If you beat the Tokyo Giants three times in a row, it can't be called a fluke."

What puzzles us is why *fluke* has become *furokku* in Japanese instead of *fuˈruˈuku, which would have been closer to the original word. The explanation must be that the word *fluke* was introduced into Japanese through the ear rather than through the eye.

fuˈru-beesu フル・ベース (lit. full base)

Furu-beesu is one of the many pseudo-loans found in Japanese baseball. Its meaning is: "bases are loaded."

(1) Wan-dan, furu-beesu desu.
    "It's one down, with bases loaded."
Furu-beesu, however, is probably not used as often as the non-loan equivalent, *man-rui.*

fu⌈ttora⌉ito フットライト (<footlights)

Footlights, meaning "the lights at the front of a stage placed at the level of the performers' feet," is *futtoraito* in Japanese. Needless to say, *futtoraito* has no plural form although, in English, *footlight* is usually used in the plural, *footlights.*

(1) Futtoraito ga kura-sugite haiyuu no kao ga yoku mienai.
    "The footlights are so dim I can't see the actors' faces very well."

Futtoraito, unlike English *footlights,* is also used figuratively in the sense of *limelight,* as in

(2) Shin-seihin ga kyuu ni futtoraito o abi-hajimeta.
    "A new product is suddenly in the limelight."

ga⌈ado ガード (<*gird*er bridge?)

There are two kinds of *gaado.* One comes from English *guard* and means "guard in sports such as basketball and football." The other *gaado,* which is being discussed here, is usually explained to have derived from *girder bridge* (see, for example, Sanseidō, p. 144). *Gaado* is a kind of overpass, almost always a railroad bridge spanning a road. According to Arakawa (p. 235), *gaʼadaa* is also used, but other dictionaries I consulted list only *gaado*.

(1) Gaado no shita o tootte mukoo-gawa ni deta.

"I passed under the overpass and came out on the other side."

gaʼarikku ガーリック (＜garlic)

The vegetable *garlic* is *ninniku,* a non-loan. When garlic is processed and made into powder, however, it is more likely to be called *gaarikku* (Japan Foundation, p. 60). In other words, a vegetable shop carries *ninniku,* but a spice shop carries *gaarikku* instead.

gaʼreʼeji ガレージ (＜garage)

Gareeji, from English *garage,* is a place for sheltering a car. The non-loan *shaʼko* "garage" probably refers to larger garages, e. g. garages owned by bus companies for sheltering buses. *Gareeji,* on the other hand, calls to mind a smaller, privately-owned garage attached to a house.

(1) Gareeji-tsuki no uchi wa Nihon de wa sukunai.

"There aren't too many houses in Japan with garages."

English *garage* may also mean "place for repairing

motor vehicles." Japanese *gareeji* cannot be used in that sense. One would have to say *ji͞do͞osha-shuurijoo* (lit. automobile repair place), which is a non-loan.

ga͞sorin-ga͞aru ガソリン・ガール (lit. gasoline girl)

Gasorin-gaaru, although not cited in too many books or dictionaries, is a pseudo-loan meaning "a young female attendant at a gas station." This is one of the many Japan-made compounds ending with *-gaaru* "girl." Some other examples are *mo͞dan-ga͞aru* (lit. modern girl), often shortened to *mo͞ga* (see *moga*), and *e͞rebeetaa-ga͞aru* (lit. elevator girl), meaning "a young female whose job is to operate an elevator."

ga͞ttsu ガッツ (<guts)

Gattsu, meaning "courage," is a recent loan used primarily in sports. According to Yoshizawa (p. 289), it is used mainly in sports such as rugby and crew as an interjection of encouragement. It is called for, I suppose, in situations where exclamations such as "Come on!" and "Hang in there!" would be uttered in English. In America, the word *guts* is used quite frequently but only as part of a sentence, and not as an interjection. Why *gattsu* became an interjection in Japanese is not clear to this author. Even now, at any rate, *gattsu* is probably not as common as non-loan exclamations of encouragement such as *Ganbare!* and *Shikkari!*, both meaning "Hang in there!"

Gutsy, the adjective form of *guts,* has not been introduced into Japanese. To mean "gutsy," therefore, one would have to use *gattsu* and add *na* (pre-noun alternant of *da*) to turn it into a pre-noun modifier, as in

(1)   gattsu na yatsu
      "a gutsy guy"

ga⌈ttsu-po⌉ozu   ガッツ・ポーズ   (lit. guts pose)

In America, when a baseball player hits a homerun or a hockey player scores a goal, he often expresses his joy by sticking out a clenched fist. This gesture was adopted by Japanese athletes in the '70s and was given the name *gattsu-poozu.*

(1)   Piito Roozu wa hoomaa o utsu to, gattsu-poozu o shite hashiri-hajimeta.
      "Pete Rose hit a homer, raised a clenched fist, and then started running."

As far as I know, there is no equivalent in English.

gera   ゲラ   (galley)

Gera, derived from *galley,* has two meanings in Japanese: (1) a long, narrow tray for holding type which has been set, and (2) galley proof. In the former sense, there is no non-loan equivalent. In the second sense, which is short for *gera-zuri* (i.e. *gera* "galley" + Japanese *zuri* "print"), it is often replaced by the non-loan synonym, *koosei-zuri* (lit. "proof print").

(1) Gera wa ashita demasu.

"The galley proof will be ready tomorrow."

go⌐o-suto⌐ppu ゴー・ストップ (lit. go-stop)

Goo-sutoppu means "traffic light." This is a pseudo-loan which was quite common in the pre-war days, although it sounds old-fashioned now. Nowadays most people would say *ko⌐otsuu-shi⌐ngoo,* a non-loan meaning "traffic signal." According to Sanseidō (p. 221), the word *goo-sutoppu* was originated from the hand-operated traffic signal common in the early Showa period (from the late '20s to the early '30s, perhaps) which consisted of written signs *Susume* "Go!" and *Tomare* "Stop!"

gu⌐riin-be⌐ruto グリーン・ベルト (<green belt)

In English, *green belt* means "an area of parks or unoccupied ground surrounding a community." This meaning has come into Japanese in the form of *guriin-beruto,* although its non-loan equivalent, *ryokuchitai* (lit. green land belt), is probably more common. In addition, unlike English *green belt,* Japanese *guriin-beruto* also means "median strip."

gu⌐riru   グリル   (＜grill)

Grill in the sense of "grillroom," i.e. "a restaurant where meats or other foods are grilled and served" was borrowed into Japanese and became *guriru,* which, however, brings to mind a slightly different image than does *grillroom. Guriru* in Japanese is sometimes used in the names of Western-style restaurants, as in *Re⌐enboo Gu⌐riru* "Rainbow Grill," and simply means "Western-style restaurant," not necessarily specializing in grilled foods.

gu⌐ro   グロ   (＜*gro*tesque)

Guro, short for *gu⌐rote⌐suku* "grotesque," is probably used at least as often as the full form because of its brevity.

(1)   Konogoro no manga wa guro ni natte-kita yoo na ki ga shimasu.

      "It seems to me that comics these days have become grotesque."

gu⌐roobu-bo⌐kkusu   グローブ・ボックス

(lit. glove box)

Guroobu-bokkusu is a pseudo-loan coined from *gu⌐ro⌐obu* "glove" and *bo⌐kkusu* "box" to mean "glove compartment." Since *ko⌐npa⌐atomento* would be both unfamiliar and too long, the shorter and more familiar *bokkusu* must have been chosen instead. This method of coining new compounds out of already familiar loans is quite common, particularly with reference to auto parts, e.g. *fu⌐ronto-ga⌐rasu* (lit. front glass, i.e. windshield) and *ba⌐kku-mi⌐raa* (lit. back mirror, i.e. rear-view mirror).

gu⌐ruupu-sa⌐unzu　グループ・サウンズ

(lit. group sounds)

Guruupu-saunzu is a pseudo-loan that refers to a rock band of three to eight members (Jiyūkokuminsha, 1976, p. 1100) or the performance of such a band (Yoshizawa & Ishiwata, p. 173). The word came into use in the late '60s, particularly after the Beatles' trip to Japan.

ha⌐adoue⌐a　ハードウエア　(<hardware)

Hardware, as in *hardware store,* corresponds to a non-loan in Japanese, i.e. *kanamono* (lit. metal thing). *Hardware store* is therefore *kanamono-ya. Haadouea* is used in Japanese only as part of the computer jargon with the meaning of "any electronic or mechanical equipment used in association with data processing." *Software* is, as might be expected, *so⌐futoue⌐a.*

ha⌐afu　ハーフ　(<half)

In addition to serving as a shorter form of *ha⌐afu-ta⌐i-mu* "half time," *ha⌐afuba⌐kku* "halfback," etc. (Miura,

p. 65), *haafu* has a fairly new meaning, i.e. "a person whose parents are of different races." Such a person used to be called by non-loans such as *ainoko* (lit. a mixed child) and *ko¬nke¬tsuji* (lit. a mixed-blooded child), but since these words carry a derogatory tone, they were consciously replaced by the newer, and therefore less biased word, *haafu.*

(1)   Ano haiyuu wa Nichi-Futsu no haafu da soo da.

      "That actor, I understand, is half Japanese and half French."

ha¬afu-ko¬oto   ハーフ・コート   (lit. half coat)

A *haafu-kooto* is a .hip-length overcoat usually for women. This is obviously a Japanese coinage. It would be called a car coat in English.

ha¬i-te¬npo   ハイ・テンポ   (lit. high tempo)

In English, one would say *quick tempo* but not **high tempo.* In Japanese, apparently by false analogy with *ha¬i-supi¬ido* "high speed," *hai-tempo* was created.

(1)   Ano hito no suru koto wa nan de mo hai-tenpo desu ne.

      "He does everything very fast, doesn't he?"

This pseudo-loan, however, is not used as often as such non-loans as *ha¬ya¬i.*

ha⌐itsu　ハイツ　(<heights)

The word *haitsu* came into Japan together with the U. S. Occupation Forces immediately after World War II. The Occupation Forces quickly established living quarters for the Occupation personnel and their families in Tokyo and named those areas Washington Heights, Palace Heights, Grant Heights, etc. The name *haitsu* was then borrowed by the Japanese when they started building housing projects for themselves.

Nowadays, however, *haitsu* is misapplied to single apartment houses. "X Haitsu" could be the name of a ritzy apartment building, not necessarily a whole housing project.

ha⌐iyaa　ハイヤー　(<hire)

Haiyaa is, according to scholars, an abbreviation of either *hired taxi* (Jiyūkokuminsha, 1976, p. 1293) or *automobile on hire* (Yoshizawa, p. 18). In any case, it refers not to a regular taxi but to a high-class taxi. Unlike regular taxis, which are either cruising around town or waiting at such places as hotels and railroad stations, a *haiyaa* stays in the garage and goes out only on demand. It is usually larger and more luxurious than a regular taxi, is hired out by the hour, and is driven by a driver in uniform. According to Yoshizawa (ibid.), the first *haiyaa* appeared in Japan about 1907.

(1)　Haiyaa o yobimashoo ka.

"Shall we call a cab from the garage?"

ha⌐nba⌐agaa   ハンバーガー   (＜hamburger)

The word *hanbaagaa* was virtually unknown in Japan until about 1971, when McDonald's opened its first Japanese restaurant in the middle of Tokyo. Since McDonald's turned out to be a great hit in Japan, *hanbaagaa* is now literally a household word for everyone. In Japanese, *hanbaagaa* means exclusively "a sandwich consisting of a hamburger steak in a roll." Unlike English *hamburger,* it never refers to uncooked ground beef.

(1) Makudonarudo e itte hanbaagaa demo tabeyoo ka.
    "Shall we go to McDonald's and eat hamburgers or something?"

ha⌐nbaagu-sute⌐eki   ハンバーグ・ステーキ
                                          (＜hamburg steak)

In English, a hamburg steak may be called by other names, e. g. a hamburger or a ground beef steak. In Japanese, a hamburg steak is called *hanbaagu-suteeki* (or *ha⌐nba⌐agu* for short) but not *ha⌐nba⌐agaa,* which is a different product (see *hanbaagaa*).

ha⌐nde   ハンデ   (＜*handi*cap)

Hande, ha⌐ndi, and *ha⌐ndikya⌐ppu* all mean "handicap." These words, of which *hande* is probably the most common variant, are most often used in sports such as golf, bowling, and horse racing.

(1) Yamada-san no gorufu wa hande nijuu da soo da.

"I hear Mr. Yamada plays golf with a handicap of 20."

In this case, there is no Japanese equivalent.

In non-sports situations, the full form, *handikyappu,* is the norm.

(2) Ano hito wa daigaku o dete-inai koto ga handikyappu ni natte-iru.

"His handicap is not having graduated from college."

In this case, *handikyappu* may be replaced by such non-loans as *fúri* "disadvantage."

haˈnsamu　ハンサム　(<handsome)

In English, *handsome* is usually a modifier for men, but it is not entirely wrong to speak of women as handsome. Moreover, *handsome* may be used for such objects as houses or furniture. In Japanese, on the other hand, *hansamu* may be used only with reference to men.

(1) Pooru Nyuuman te hansamu nee!

"Isn't Paul Newman handsome?"

There are non-loans that could be used to refer to good-looking men such as *bíˈnan* (lit. beautiful man), *bíˈnaˈnshi* (more or less synonymous with *binan*), *otoko-mae* (lit. manly looks), but *hansamu* is the most colloquial and the most up-to-date expression at present.

han-suto ハン・スト (<*hun*ger *st*rike)

Han-suto is short for *ha⌐ngaa-sutora⌐iki*. Since the full form is very long, the shorter form is much more common, especially in writing. *Han-suto* could also be called *da⌐n-jiki-su⌐to, danjiki* being a non-loan meaning "fasting," but this latter form is not as common as *han-suto*.

Han-suto should be clearly distinguished from *pan-suto*, which means "pantihose" (see *pan-suto*).

hau-tsuu-mono ハウ・ツウもの (<how-to+Japanese *mono* "thing")

Hau-tsuu-mono is a combination of *hau-tsuu* "how-to" and Japanese *mono* "thing." It means "how-to book."
(1) Konogoro wa hau-tsuu-mono ga hayatte-imasu.
  "These days how-to books are popular."
For some reason, *how-to book* did not become **ha⌐u-tsuu-bu⌐kku* in Japanese—a puzzling phenomenon.

He⌐bon ヘボン (<Hepburn)

The name *Hebon* is familiar to most Japanese and most students of Japanese as part of *Hebon-shiki*, meaning "the Hepburn system," a system of romanization applied to the Japanese language.

Hebon refers to James Curtis Hepburn, an American missionary-doctor who came to Japan in 1859 and stayed until 1892. During that time, he opened the first Japanese charity hospital, compiled the first Japanese-English dictionary, and founded an English school, which later developed into today's Meiji Gakuin University. For his dictionary (1886), he devised a romanization system, which, after some adaptations, came to be known as *He⌐bon-shiki rooma⌐ji* "Hepburn-system romanization." This system is still widely used today, especially for railroad signs and Japanese-English dictionaries.

The fact James Curtis Hepburn is known as Hebon in Japanese shows that effort was made either by him or by people around him to preserve the original pronunciation of his name as much as possible. The spelling was therefore totally ignored. It is worthy of note that, later on in the 20th century, when two other Hepburns, both movie actresses, became well-known in Japan, i. e. Katherine Hepburn and Audrey Hepburn, their last names both came to be known not as *Hebon,* but as *He⌐ppuba⌐an,* which was definitely a spelling-based pronunciation.

hi⌐era⌐rukii ヒエラルキー （＜hierarchy）

Hierarukii is actually a hybrid between German *Hierarchie* and English *hierarchy. Hieraru-* comes from the first part of the German word, and *-kii* from the last part of the English. It is very likely that German *Hierarchie* first came into Japanese and became *hi⌈era⌉ruhii,* which later, under the influence of English *hierarchy,* changed into *hierarukii,* but this is all a pure conjecture on my part.

Kōjien and Arakawa list both *hieraruhii* and *hierarukii,* while Sanseidō and Yoshizawa list only *hierarukii.*

As is the case with English *hierarchy,* Japanese *hierarukii* means "a system of persons ranked one above another, as in bureaucracy or the military." This is a highly intellectual word in Japanese used exclusively by the well-educated, particularly by scholars. There are some non-loans with similar meanings, e.g. *ka⌈ikyuu-so⌉-shiki* and *kaisoo-sei,* both meaning "class system."

hiyaringu ヒヤリング (<hearing)

Hiyaringu (or *hiaringu*), from English *hearing,* has a very specialized meaning: "hearing as one of the skills taught in a foreign language class."

(1) Ano hito no Eigo wa hiyaringu ga joozu da kedo, hanasu to machigai ga ooi desu.

"His hearing skill in English is very good, but he makes many errors when he speaks."

ho⌈chikisu ホチキス (<Hotchkiss)

A stapler could be called *su⌈te⌉epuraa* in Japanese.

At least, the word appears in most dictionaries, but I am positive that the instrument is much better known as *hochikisu* to most Japanese. *Hochikisu* is derived from the name of B. B. Hotchkiss (1826-86), an American who invented the stapler as well as the rifle and the machine gun.

(1) Sumimasen ga hochikisu o kashite-kudasai.

"Excuse me, but may I borrow your stapler?"

ho͞ippu-kuri͞imu ホイップ・クリーム

(＜*whip*ped *cream*)

Whipped cream is known in Japanese as *hoippu-kuriimu*. As is the case with other loanwords such as *ko͞ndensu-mi͞ruku* "*condense*d *milk*" and *ko͞on-bi͞ifu* "*corn*ed *beef*," the past participle ending was dropped in the process of borrowing. The full form *ho͞ipputo-kuri͞imu* is probably not as common. There is no non-loan equivalent.

ho͞iru ホイル （＜foil)

Hoiru, from *foil,* has only one meaning, i. e., "a very thin aluminum sheet used for cooking." Another version, which is a little closer to the original pronunciation, is *fo͞iru.* Which to use is entirely a matter of individual preference. There is no non-loan equivalent.

(1) Osakana wa hoiru (*or* foiru) ni tsutsunde oobun ni

oire-kudasai.

"Please put the fish in the oven after wrapping it in foil."

ho˥n ホン (<phon)

Hon or *fo˥n* is from English *phon,* a unit for measuring the loudness of a sound. In Japan, *hon* is the regular unit although, in America, decibels are used instead. A normal conversation is measured at 40 *hon,* and human ears cannot stand loudness above 120 *hon* (Sanseidō, p. 668).

(1) Ano koosaten no rasshu-awaa no onryoo wa hyaku-hon-gurai desu.

"The amount of noise during rush hours at that intersection is about 100 phons."

ho˥omu-be˥esu ホーム・ベース (lit. home base)

In American baseball, *home base* sounds a little obsolete. *Plate* or *home plate* is more common (Hani, pp. 32-33). In Japanese baseball, on the other hand, *hoomu-beesu* "home base" is probably still as common as *ho˥o-mu-pure˥eto.*

ho˥omu˥-in ホーム・イン (lit. home-in)

This is another pseudo-loan very commonly used in

Japanese baseball. It means "reaching home."

(1) Pitchaa wairudo-pitchi, rannaa san-rui kara hoomu-in!

"The pitcher delivers a wild pitch; the runner scores from third."

Reaching the finish line in a race is called *go⌐oru⌐-in* (lit. goal-in) in Japanese. *Hoomu-in* follows the same kind of word formation. Since a runner's goal is not *go⌐oru* but *ho⌐omu* in baseball, reaching home is naturally *hoomu-in.*

ho⌐omu-ro⌐on　ホーム・ローン　(<home loan)

Hoomu-roon means "home loan," i.e. a loan you take out to buy or build a home. Another variant, which is just as common is *ju⌐utaku-ro⌐on,* i.e. Japanese *juutaku* "residence"+*ro⌐on* "loan."

(1) Konogoro wa hoomu-roon mo rishi ga takakute taihen desu nee.

"The interest rate on home loans has gotten out of hand these days, hasn't it?"

Hoomu-roon is not a pseudo-loan as claimed by Yoshizawa (p. 192). It comes directly from English *home loan.*

ho⌐suto-ku⌐rabu　ホスト・クラブ　(lit. host club)

The Women's Lib movement has invaded Japan, too!

There are night spots called *hosuto-kurabu,* which are specifically for women. They are bars where "hosts," i. e. male companions, entertain female customers.

ho⌐tto-do⌐ggu   ホット・ドッグ   (<hot dog)

In English, *hot dog* means both "frankfurter" and "sandwich consisting of a frankfurter in a split roll." Japanese *hotto-doggu* can mean only the latter. A frankfurter by itself is not a *hotto-doggu,* but a *fu⌐rankufuruto-soose⌐eji* (see *furankufuruto-sooseeji*).

(1) Hotto-doggu o futatsu mo tabeta no de, onaka ga ippai ni narimashita.

     "I ate two hot dogs and became completely full."

ho⌐waito-ri⌐kaa   ホワイト・リカー   (lit. white liquor)

In Japan, there is a cheap distilled liquor called *sho-⌐ochu⌐u,* which traditionally has been enjoyed by the hoi poloi. The word *shoochuu* therefore carries a low-class image with it. Recently, in their effort to push up the sales of *shoochuu,* liquor companies have started calling it *howaito-rikaa.* The liquor itself has not changed, but the new name certainly makes *shoochuu* sound like a more modern and desirable product. Whether or not it is because of the new name, the sales of *shoochuu* are going up, and even middle-class people are now drinking it.

hyu⌐uzu ヒューズ (<fuse)

Hyuuzu and *fyu⌐uzu* both come from English *fuse* meaning "a piece of metal that melts when there is excess current in the circuit." *Hyuuzu* is definitely more widely used than *fyuuzu,* which is closer to the pronunciation of the original word. In other words, both *fuse* and *Hughes* (as in *Howard Hughes*) are pronounced the same way in Japanese.

(1) Mata hyuuzu ga tonde denki ga kiete-shimatta.
"The fuse has blown again, and the lights are out."

i⌐ijii-o⌐odaa イージー・オーダー (lit. easy order)

Iijii-oodaa is a pseudo-loan used by the garment industry. It refers to the method of tailoring a suit (mostly men's) without a fitting, thus cutting down the cost. *Iijii-oodaa* was publicized particularly by large department stores, and was quite popular from about 1949 to 1965 (Yoshizawa and Ishiwata, pp. 50-51). Customers were usually not given a choice of fabrics or styles, but the suits were of course made to their measurements. Nowadays, *iijii-oodaa,* or *iijii-meedo* (lit. easy made), is losing ground because of the much wider range of high-quality ready-made suits available.

i⌐ndian-pe⌐epaa インディアン・ペーパー
(lit. Indian paper)

Thin, opaque paper used particularly for dictionaries

is often called *indian-peepaa* in Japanese by mistake, although *índia-peépaa* "India paper" is also used. *Indian-peepaa* must have been coined by someone who knew that the adjective form of *India* is *Indian*; he therefore went on to "correct" the original form. This is truly a good example of "A little knowledge is a dangerous thing."

ínisharu　イニシャル　(<initial)

Japanese *inisharu*, although it stems from *initial*, does not have all the meanings of the original English word. In fact, it means only one thing, i.e. "the romanized initials of one's name." For example, if you buy a suit or have one made in Japan, you may be asked the following question:

(1)　Inisharu o otsuke-shimashoo ka.
　　　"Shall we embroider your initials [on the lining]?"

ínku　インク　(<ink)

Apparently, ink was first introduced to Japan by the Dutch during the Edo Period; therefore Dutch *inkt* was the name the Japanese learned first, pronouncing it *ínki-to,* or *ínki* for short. The version *inkito* was short-lived, partly because of the influence of the English word *ink,* which the Japanese learned next in the mid-19th century, after ending their long isolation. Nowadays, ink is known as either *inki* or *inku,* the latter obviously coming from English *ink.* In fact, *inku* is becoming more and more common than *inki,* which is beginning to sound a little old-fashioned.

(1) Inku wa ao ga ichiban futsuu deshoo.

"Blue is probably the most common color for ink."

ja⌐a ジャー (<jar)

In English, a jar is a broad-mouthed container. Peanut butter, for example, is usually sold in a jar. In Japanese, on the other hand, *jaa,* although it is derived from English *jar,* means something entirely different, i.e. a large thermos bottle, which is known in America as an air pot. A smaller thermos bottle, however, is not a *jaa* but a *ma⌐ho⌐o-bin,* a non-loan which literally means "magic bottle."

(1) Kono jaa wa asa atsui oyu o irete-oku to, ban made hiemasen.

"If you pour boiling hot water into this air pot in the morning, it is still hot in the evening."

ja⌐ajii ジャージー (<jersey)

Although *jaajii* comes from *jersey,* these two words refer to different things. English *jersey* refers to a close-fitting knitted sweater or shirt worn by seamen, athletes, etc., or a similar knitted garment worn by women. In

Japanese, on the other hand, *jaajii* usually means "jersey cloth," i. e. a kind of fabric. When *jaajii* refers to a knitted garment, it refers specifically to a shirt worn by ruggers.

ja⌐jji　ジャッジ　(<judge)

Jajji in Japanese never refers to a judge in a court of law. It is used only in the sense of judge in a competition, contest, or sports event, especially if it is Western-style.
(1)　Bokushingu no matchi ni wa futsuu jajji ga nan-nin iru n desu ka.
　　　"How many judges are there usually at a boxing match?"

jaketsu　ジャケツ　(<jacket)

According to Yoshizawa (p. 77), *jaketsu* means "a knitted sweater, cardigan, etc." This use is probably obsolete. Nowadays a sweater is always called *se⌐etaa* (or *su⌐e⌐etaa*), and a cardigan is called *ka⌐adigan*. Most young people probably don't use the word *jaketsu* any more. (Also see *jaketto*.)

ja⌐ketto　ジャケット　(<jacket)

Jaketto, like *jaketsu,* comes from English *jacket,* but whereas *jaketsu* has become obsolete, *jaketto* is still very much alive, especially in compounds such as *su-*⌐*pootsu-ja*⌐*ketto* (<sports jacket) and *da*⌐*un-ja*⌐*ketto* (< down jacket). A jacket that constitutes part of a suit, however, is never referrred to as *jaketto* but always as *uwagi,* a non-loan.

Jaketto (but not *jaketsu*) also means "a paper or card-board envelope for protecting a phonograph record." There is no non-loan equivalent.

(1) Kono rekoodo no jaketto wa chotto sekushii-sugi-
       masu nee.

       "Isn't the jacket of this record a little too sexy?"

A jacket for a book may also be called *jaketto,* but more often it is referred to as *ka*⌐*baa* (<cover).

ja⌐**npaa** ジャンパー (<jumper)

Japanese *janpaa* has two meanings. First, it means "athlete whose specialty is jumping, as in track or skiing." Second, it is a kind of jacket, usually with a zippered front and closely fit at the wrists and the waist. The kind of leather jacket worn by members of motorcycle gangs is known as *ka*⌐*wa-ja*⌐*npaa* (<Japanese *ka*⌐*wa*⌐ "leather" +*janpaa* "jumper"), or *kawa-jan* for short.

English *jumper,* when it refers to clothing, usually means a one-piece, sleeveless dress or a skirt with straps and a complete or partial bodice, usually worn over a blouse by women and children. In Japan, however, this kind of clothing is referred to as *ja*⌐*npaa-suka*⌐*ato* (lit.

jumper skirt), a pseudo-loan created probably to make a distinction between this type of clothing and a kind of jacket called *janpaa,* as described in the above paragraph.

ji¯mu　ジム　(<gym)

English *gym* is short for *gymnasium,* meaning "a building or room designed and equipped for physical education activities." The Japanese counterpart is usually *taïïkukan,* a non-loan composed of *taïiku* "physical education" and *ka¯n* "hall, *or* building." The loanword *jimu,* which comes from English *gym,* has a very specialized meaning: "a gym for boxing."

(1) Mainichi taiikukan de basuketto o yatte-imasu.
"I play basketball in the gym every day."

(2) Ano hito wa kono hen no jimu de bokushingu o naratte-iru soo desu.
"I hear he is learning boxing at a nearby boxing club."

It was the short form, *gym,* that came into the Japanese vocabulary, not the full form, *gymnasium.*

ji¯nkusu　ジンクス　(<jinx)

English *jinx* means "a person, thing, or influence supposed to bring bad luck." Japanese *jinkusu,* however, is used with reference to not only bad luck but good luck as well. In the following examples, therefore, only the first use of *jinkusu* actually reflects the correct use of the original English word.

(1) Shiai no mae ni hige o soru to makeru to iu jinkusu o shinjite-iru tenisu-senshu ga iru.

"There are some tennis players who believe that they will be jinxed if they shave before a match."

(2) Shiai no mae ni hige o soranai to iu *jinkusu* o mamotte-iru tenisu-senshu ga iru.

"There are some tennis players who observe the practice of not shaving before a match, hoping that will bring good luck (lit. tennis players who observe the *jinx of not shaving...)."

As the translations of the above examples show, only in example (1) does *jinkusu* correspond to *jinx*.

jo̅kki ジョッキ (<jug)

Japanese *jokki,* derived from *jug,* is a little different in meaning from the original English word, for it refers exclusively to a large glass with a handle to drink beer from, not to pour beer from.

The fact that *jug* yielded *jokki,* and not *ja̅ggu,* as it would have if the word had been borrowed recently, shows that it was introduced into Japanese quite some time ago. Sure enough, Sanseidō (p. 312) classifies *jokki* as a Meiji borrowing.

(1) Ano bia-hooru no jokki wa zuibun ookii desu yo.

"That beer hall serves beer in large mugs (*or* steins)."

ju⌐usu ジュース (<juice, deuce)

Japanese *juusu,* from English *juice,* is somewhat different in meaning from the latter. Like English *juice,* Japanese *juusu* may refer to fruit juice or vegetable juice, but unlike English *juice,* Japanese *juusu* might also mean "a drink prepared by adding sugar, water, and other additives to fruit juice." In any case, in Japanese, *juusu* has to be a beverage. Meat juice, therefore, cannot be called *juusu* in Japanese.

(1) Mainichi yasai-juusu o nomu no wa karada ni yoi.
    "Drinking vegetable juice every day is good for the health."

ka⌐ateru カーテル (lit. *car*+ho*tel*)

Passin reports that he has seen the word *kaateru* (p. 167). *Kaateru* is obviously patterned after *mo⌐oteru,* which was derived from English *motel,* which in turn was formed from *motor* and *hotel.* English *motel* has some variants such as *motor court* and *tourist court.* None of these variants, however, has ever come into Japanese. Instead, some "creative" Japanese apparently decided to coin a new variant by putting together *ka⌐a* "car" and *teru* "ho*tel*," thus creating *kaateru.*

ka⌐me カメ (<Come here!)

In early Meiji, *kame,* or *ka⌐meya,* was sometimes used to mean "Western dog (i.e. a dog of Western breed)." Since Japanese *kame* normally means "turtle" or "tortoise," one may very well wonder how the same word could possibly have come to mean "dog" also. Actually, however, *kame* meaning "Western dog" is a loan-word and has nothing to do with Japanese *kame,* meaning "turtle" or "tortoise." In fact, the loanword *kame* was derived from English "Come here!" In early Meiji, when Americans and Britishers started coming to Japan, some of them brought dogs along. Japanese people, hearing these dog owners yell out "Come here!" to their dogs, surmised that it must be the English equivalent of Japanese *i⌐nu⌐* "dog." These Japanese, who were unfamiliar with English, heard "Come here!" as *Kameya.* Now, in those days, it was quite customary for Japanese people to call out to their dogs and cats by adding *-ya* to the name, *-ya* being a vocative suffix. For example, if a dog's name was *Kuro* "Blackie," his owner would call out *Kuro-ya!* ("Blackie!") to beckon him. By false analogy, therefore, *ya* in *Kameya* was interpreted by some people as the same vocative ending as *-ya* in *Kuro-ya,* and was thus dropped to yield *kame* (Umegaki, 1975b, pp. 186-88)!

The loanword *kame* has since become obsolete and is no longer used (except that in the Akita dialect a mutt that barks indiscriminately was referred to as *kame-inu* as late as in 1954, according to Arakawa, p. 272). Nowadays, *yooken,* a non-loan, is the word for "Western dog." I am citing *kame* here, however, as an illustration of how unpredictably idiosyncratic a loanword could be.

ka⌐mera⌐ カメラ (<camera)

When I was a child, a camera was still called a *sha-⌐shi⌐nki,* I believe. Nowadays, however, *shashinki* sounds absolutely outdated. Most Japanese, except very old people, prefer *kamera* to *shashinki.* Nishio (p. 166) claims that there might even be a slight difference in meaning between the two: while *kamera* suggests a new high-quality camera, *shashinki* calls to mind an old-fashioned box-type camera.

(1) Megane o kakete kamera o ni-dai burasagete-iru
    Tooyoo-jin no kankookyaku wa daitai Nihon-jin
    da to iwarete-iru.

    "They say that Oriental tourists wearing glasses and toting two cameras are almost always Japanese."

ka⌐mera-fe⌐esu カメラ・フェース (lit. camera face)

Kamera-feesu is a pseudo-loan composed of *ka⌐mera* "camera" and *fe⌐esu* "face," and means "one's face as seen in a photograph."

(1) Ano hito wa anmari bijin da to omowanai ga,
    kamera-feesu ga ii.

"I don't think she is really beautiful, but she has a photogenic face (lit. she has a good camera face)."

In more traditional Japanese, one would say *ka͞mera-u͞tsuri ga ii* (lit. [she] looks good in photos) instead.

ka͞muba͞kku　カムバック　(<comeback)

Comeback in English means "return to a former rank, popularity, position, prosperity, etc." Japanese *kamubakku,* from English *comeback,* means the same thing, but it mainly applies to a limited number of fields, especially sports, entertainment, or politics.

(1) Ano joyuu wa nan-nen mo byooki datta ga, kondo kamubakku-shita.

"That actress, who was sick for many years, staged a comeback recently."

(2) Intai-shita Oh-senshu no kamubakku o kitai-shite mo muda da.

"It's useless to expect a comeback from Oh, who has retired."

In English, there can be other much less grandiose kinds of comeback. For example, if a tennis player who is behind 0-5 in a set suddenly starts playing well and evens the score at 5-5, his opponent might congratulate him, saying "Good comeback!" Japanese *kamubakku* is never used for a minor occasion like that.

Kamubakku has a non-loan equivalent *kaerizaki,* but the former is probably more common than the latter.

Kamubakku also has another version, *ka⌐nba⌐kku.*

ke⌐esu-bai-ke⌐esu ケース・バイ・ケース
(＜case by case)

Keesu-bai-keesu is a rather unusual loanword in that not just one English word but one whole phrase made up of three words was borrowed as a unit.

(1) Soo yuu mondai wa keesu-bai-keesu de shori-sureba ii daroo.

"Those matters should be handled on a case by case basis."

This loanword is probably used mostly by people who have a good knowledge of English or who want to show themselves off as knowledgeable.

ko⌐in-ra⌐ndorii コイン・ランドリー (lit. coin laundry)

Commercial laundries with coin-operated washers and driers are usually known as laundromats, launderettes, and such in the United States, but in Japan they are called *koin-randorii.*

According to Fukao (pp. 30-31), although the first Japanese *koin-randorii* did not open until 1971, there were already 3,500 of them in 1979, most of which were concentrated in big cities such as Tokyo, Osaka, and Nagoya. She says that, of the 1,690 in Tokyo (also as of 1979), 735 were run by public bath houses, which means that many people take baths while getting their wash done—a uniquely Japanese phenomenon!

(1) Uchi ni sentakuki no nai hito wa koin-randorii o tsukaeba ii deshoo.

"People who don't have washers at home could use coin-operated laundries."

ko⌐mi⌐sshon コミッション (<commission)

Komisshon, from English *commission*, is known to most Japanese in one sense only, i.e. "a sum or percentage allowed to an agent, salesman, etc., for his service." This use is stretched in Japanese, however, so that *komisshon* is sometimes used as a euphemism for the non-loan *wa⌐iro* "bribe."

ko⌐mon-se⌐nsu コモン・センス (<common sense)

Komon-sensu, although derived from English *common sense*, is not exactly the same as the latter. While *common sense* signifies "sound practical judgment" or "normal native intelligence," *komon-sensu* is generally used as the equivalent of the non-loan *jooshiki*, which means "general knowledge," i.e. "something that everyone is supposed to know." *Komon-sensu* is not used as often as *jooshiki*.

ko⌐npa コンパ (<*compa*ny)

Konpa comes from English *company*. While *company* has many meanings, *konpa* has only one, i.e. "a social gathering where food and beverages are served on a Dutch treat basis." The word is almost exclusively used by students.

(1) Kimatsu-shiken ga owattara konpa o shiyoo.

"Let's have a party after the final exams."

A *konpa,* though translated as *party* in the above example, is not the kind of party American students are accustomed to. At a *konpa,* there is usually a lot of friendly conversation, but often the whole group participates in it together instead of breaking up into smaller groups. There is a lot of eating and drinking, and sometimes singing too, but rarely dancing.

ko⌐npa⌐hion コンパニオン (<companion)

Konpanion, from English *companion,* came into use at the Tokyo Olympiad of 1964 in the sense of "woman interpreter-guide for foreign visitors." At the Osaka Expo of 1970, more *konpanion* were hired for the same purpose of helping foreigners. Nowadays, according to Fukao (p. 130), there is a new pseudo-loan *go⌐rufu-konpa⌐nion* (lit. golf companion), which is a euphemism for good-looking women caddies hired as a gimmick by a new golf club!

ko⌐npe コンペ (<*compe*tition)

Konpe, from English *competition,* refers mainly to two types of competition. One is a public competition for architectural designs. The other, which is far more common, is a golf competition.

(1) Kondo no nichiyoo wa shanai-konpe ga aru kara, ichinichi rusu-suru yo.

"There's a company golf meet next Sunday, so I'll be gone all day."

In the latter sense, *konpe* is probably more common in speech while its non-loan counterpart, *kyo⌐ogi⌐kai,* is more often used as a written form.

ko⌐npyuutaa-are⌐rugii コンピューター・アレルギー
(<computer + German *Allergie*)

Konpyuutaa-arerugii is a hybrid from *ko⌐npyu⌐utaa* (<English *computer*) and *a⌐re⌐rugii* (<German *Allergie* "allergy") and means "computer phobia." According to Jiyūkokuminsha (1976, p. 746), this "disease" is brought about by a lack of familiarity with computers or by a fear that computers might take over jobs currently occupied by humans. *Konpyuutaa-arerugii* is more or less synonymous with *ko⌐npyu⌐utaa-kyoofushoo* (<*konpyuutaa*+non-loan *kyoofushoo,* meaning "phobia").

(1) Amerika no roodoosha no naka ni wa konpyuutaa-arerugii ni kakatte-iru mono mo sukunaku nai.

"Among American laborers, there are some who are suffering from 'computer phobia.'"

ko⌐nsa⌐isu コンサイス (<concise)

Konsaisu, from English *concise,* conjures up only one image in the mind of an average Japanese, i.e. the image of a small dictionary. The reason is because Sanseidō, a publishing house, started publishing in the Taisho period a series of dictionaries, small in size but fairly high in quality, which were all named *Konsaisu Such and Such,* e.g. *Ko⌐nsaisu Eiwa Ji⌐ten* (lit. Concise English-Japanese Dictionary) and *Ko⌐nsaisu Waei Ji⌐ten* (lit. Concise Japanese-English Dictionary). This series became such a great hit that today, after many revisions, it is still extremely popular and widely used. As a result, although *Konsaisu* was originally a brand name, similar dictionaries published by other publishers may also be referred to as *Konsaisu-ban* (lit. Concise edition).

kontena コンテナ (<container)

Kontena, from English *container,* is not just any kind of container but one specific kind, i.e. the kind of container used for shipment of freight by container car or container ship. (Other kinds of containers such as cartons, crates, and cans are never called *kontena* in Japanese.)

Containerization, which revolutionalized freight shipment, has become popular in Japan also and is referred to as *ko⌐ntenarize⌐eshon.*

There seems to be a new trend in Japanese to make long vowels in loanwords somewhat shorter. *Container,* for example, would have normally yielded **konteenaa,* but it has become *kontena* instead (although *kontenaa* seems to be a permissible variant). *K⌐onpyu⌐utaa* (from *computer*) also has a shorter variant, *k⌐onpyu⌐uta.*

ko⌐ochaazu-bo⌐kkusu コーチャーズ・ボックス
(lit. coacher's box)

In baseball, there are boxes next to first and third bases where coaches stand to give instructions to base runners and batters. These boxes are often called *koochaazu-bokkusu* in Japanese, lit. "coacher's box." Lately, however, the trend is from *koochaazu-bokkusu* to *ko⌐ochizu-bo⌐kkusu* "coach's box." The latter is probably a better reflection of English.

ko⌐orudo-ge⌐emu コールド・ゲーム (lit. called game)

Koorudo-geemu is a baseball term meaning "a game called because of such factors as darkness and bad weather after the fifth inning is over." Unlike a *no⌐o-ge⌐emu* (see *noo-geemu*), a *koorudo-geemu* counts as a regulation game.

ko⌐ramu コラム (<column)

Koramu has only one meaning: "a newspaper column," especially a column which has a readily identifiable heading and comments upon a particular field of interest." "Tensei-jingo (i.e. Vox Populi, Vox Dei)" in the *Asahi* newspaper is probably the most well-known *koramu*.

ko⌐re⌐kutaa コレクター (<collector)

Collectors of antiques and art objects are usually called *shuushuuka*, a non-loan, but sometimes *korekutaa*. Ishiwata (p. 140) also cites a pseudo-loan *ko⌐re⌐kushonaa* (lit. collectioner), which was obviously coined by adding *aa* (from English *-or*) to *ko⌐re⌐kushon* (<collection), but as he rightly states, there is of course no such English word as **collectioner*. Fortunately, however, *korekushonaa* is not listed in any of the dictionaries I consulted; this incorrect version, therefore, cannot be very common.

A maniacal collector is usually referred to as a *shuu-shuu-kyoo*, a non-loan literally meaning "collection-maniac." There is a pseudo-loan for this, too, i.e. *ko⌐re-kuto-ma⌐nia* (lit. collect mania).

kuchi-komi ロコミ (<Japanese *kuchi* "mouth" +
                                   *commu*nication)

Kuchi-komi is a hybrid made up of Japanese *kuchi*

and the loanword *komi* (short for *ko⌐myunike⌐eshon,* from English *communication*), and means "communication by word of mouth"). According to Jiyūkokuminsha (1976, p. 994), the word implies the power of rumor.

(1) Kuchi-komi no iryoku wa baka ni dekinai.

  "The power of rumor is nothing to sneeze at."

Kuchi-komi is different from the non-loan *uwasa* "rumor" in that it sounds more up-to-date and desirable than the latter.

ku⌐rashikku-pa⌐ntsu クラシック・パンツ

(lit. classic pants)

This pseudo-loan, coined as a euphemism by a weekly magazine for men (Sanseidō, p. 186), means "E⌐tchuu-fu⌐ndoshi," i.e. a kind of loincloth Japanese men used to wear under a kimono. Nowadays most Japanese men have switched to Western-style underpants. As a result, despite the new coinage, not many *Etchuu-fundoshi* are being worn any more.

ku⌐riimu-so⌐oda クリーム・ソーダ

($<$ice-*cream soda*)

After ice-cream soda was first introduced to Japan, the name *a⌐isu-kuriimu-so⌐oda* was shortened to *kuriimu-sooda,* which is far more common now. What most Japanese speakers don't realize, however, is that English *cream soda* refers not to ice-cream soda but to a soft drink made with vanilla-flavored, carbonated water colored brown by caramel. When a Japanese visitor to America wishes to order ice-cream soda, therefore, he must specifically ask for "ice-cream soda" and not for "cream soda"!

ku⌐riin'appu-to⌐rio　クリーンアップ・トリオ
(lit. cleanup trio)

In American baseball, *cleanup* means "the fourth position or person in the batting order," as in "So-and-so is batting cleanup today." In Japan, the word was misapplied and became part of a new compound *kuriin'-appu-torio* which refers not only to the fourth but to the third and fifth batters as well.

(1) Ano chiimu no kuriin'appu-torio wa sugoi.

　　　lit. "That team has a tremendous 'cleanup trio,'"

　　　i. e. "That team has tremendous hitters in the third, fourth, and fifth positions."

Another variant is *ku⌐riinnappu-to⌐rio,* which means exactly the same thing.

ku⌐ro⌐oku　クローク　(<*cloak*room)

Cloakroom is *ku⌐rookuru⌐umu* in Japanese, but since *kurookuruumu* is a long word, it is often abbreviated to just *kurooku,* as in

(1) Watashi konogoro ano hoteru no kurooku de aru-
   baito-shite-iru n desu.
   "I'm working part-time in the cloakroom of that
   hotel these days."

ku⌐ro¬oru クロール (<crawl)

Kurooru means "crawl" only in one sense, i. e. a
kind of stroke used in swimming.
(1) Boku wa hiraoyogi wa dekiru keredo, kurooru wa
   zenzen dame na n desu.
   "I can do the breaststroke, but I'm not at all good
   at the crawl."

For the regular meaning of crawl, i. e. "to move
close to the ground like a worm or on hands and knees
like a little child," the non-loan *ha⌐u¬* is used, as in
(2) Uchi no akanboo wa yatto hau yoo ni narimashita.
   "Our baby has finally started crawling."

ku⌐ro¬ozu-a⌐ppu クローズ・アップ (<close-up)

Close-up is an Americanism meaning "a picture taken
at close range to permit a close and detailed view of an
object." Since it comes from the adverbial phrase *close
up,* in which *close* is pronounced [klous], it should have
yielded **ku⌐ro¬osu-a⌐ppu* in Japanese. However, *close* in
close-up was misidentified in Japan with the verb *close,*
which is pronounced [klouz]. Thus the loanword *kuroozu-appu* was born.

(1) Joyuu no kuroozu-appu-sareta kao ga sukuriin
    ippai ni utsutta.
    "A close shot of the actress's face filled the whole
    screen."

Kuroozu-appu is also used figuratively to refer to
something that is highlighted, as in

(2) Koogai-mondai ga ookiku kuroozu-appu-sarete-
    kita no wa senkyuuhyakurokujuu-nen-dai datta
    daroo.
    "It must have been in the 1960's that the issue of
    environmental pollution was brought to the fore."

ku⌐rosu-ge¬emu クロス・ゲーム (＜close game)

When I first heard the word *kurosu-geemu* as a
youngster, I identified *kurosu* with English *cross* and
thought that *kurosu-geemu* must refer to a game in which
the lead changed hands time and time again since *cross*
could mean "to pass from one side to another." Of course
I was wrong. *Kurosu-geemu* actually comes from English
close game, which should have yielded **ku⌐roosu-ge¬emu.*
For some reason, however, the shorter *kurosu* was a-
dopted instead.

ku⌐rosu-pure¬e クロス・プレー (＜close play)

This is a baseball term originated from English *close
play,* which, as in the case of *close game,* should have

yielded *$ku^\lceil roosu$-$pure^\rceil e$. Many Japanese baseball players and fans, as I did once myself, probably misidentify *kurosu* with English *cross* instead of *close* and mistakenly think that *kurosu-puree* is so called because, in a close play, the players involved often *cross* each other's path!

ku⌐uraa クーラー (lit. cooler)

Although *The Random House Dictionary of the English Language* lists "an air-conditioner" as one of the meanings of *cooler,* the word is usually used in America to refer to a container in which something may be kept cool as in "Let's take the cooler on tomorrow's picnic with some beer and coke." Japanese *kuuraa,* on the other hand, means nothing but "air-conditioner."

(1) Kono heya wa kuuraa ga kiki-sugite samui desu nee.
    "The air-conditioner in this room is turned up too high. I feel cold, don't you?"

kya⌐betsu キャベツ (＜cabbage)

According to Arakawa (p. 318), cabbage was first grown in Japan in 1871, the fourth year of Meiji. As was the case with early-Meiji loanwords, *cabbage* must have been borrowed aurally. A spelling-based borrowing would have yielded *$kya^\lceil beeji$ instead.

(1) Nihon no kyabetsu wa Amerika no kyabetsu to chotto chigau soo desu ne.

"Is it true that Japanese cabbage is a little different from American cabbage?"

kya⌐npingu-kaa⌐ キャンピング・カー

(lit. camping car)

The type of recreational vehicle used by campers is called a camper in the United States, but a *kyanpingu-kaa* in Japan. *Kya⌐npaa,* from English *camper,* does not refer to recreational vehicles in Japan probably because, prior to the introduction of such recreational vehicles, the word had been used for a long time to mean "a person who camps out for recreation." Extending the meaning of the same word would have only created confusion.

(1) Nihon de wa mada kyanpingu-kaa wa amari ooku arimasen.

"In Japan, not too many people own campers yet."

kya⌐npu⌐-in キャンプ・イン (lit. camp in)

Kyanpu-in is a pseudo-loan meaning "reporting to training camp," particularly with reference to spring training for professional baseball players.

(1) Kyojin-gun wa kinoo Furorida de kyanpu-in-shi-mashita.

"The Tokyo Giants arrived at their spring training site in Florida yesterday."

The word order of *kyanpu-in* precisely follows the Japanese word order for *kyańpu ni hairu* "to report to camp." The same word order is followed in other pseudo-loans ending with *-in* such as *gooru⌐in* "reaching the finish line in a race," *ho⌐omu⌐in* "reaching home in base-ball," and *be⌐ddo⌐-in* "going to bed together."

kya⌐ppu   キャップ   (<cap, *cap*tain)

Kyappu, from *cap,* mostly refers to the cap of a pen.

(1)   Mannenhitsu no kyappu o nakushite-shimatta.

"I've lost the cap of my fountain pen."

Kyappu is also used by the press to refer to someone heading a team of reporters. In this case, *kyappu* is short for English *captain.*

kya⌐tchi-ba⌐a   キャッチ・バー   (lit. catch bar)

Kyatchi-baa is a fairly new pseudo-loan coined from *catch* plus *bar.* The word refers to bars that "catch" passers-by, bring them in by force, and serve them liquor at exhorbitant prices.

(1)   Shinjuku-sho wa kyatchi-baa no torishimari ni noridashita.

"The Shinjuku Police Station has launched an of-fensive to control the 'catch bars.'"

LDK ($<$ *l*iving room, *d*ining room, *k*itchen)

According to Yoshizawa and Ishiwata (p. 93), *LDK* (pronounced "e⌐ru-dii-kee⌐") was first coined by Nihon Jūtaku Kōdan ("The Japan Housing Corporation"), probably in the 1960's to refer to a room which serves as a combination living room, dining room, and kitchen.

maagarin マーガリン ($<$margarine)

Margarine is called *maagarin* in Japanese, which shows that the word must have been introduced first as a written form. If it had been introduced through the ear, it would have become *maajerin in Japanese. But how can we blame the person, whoever he was, who was responsible for distorting the pronunciation of the original word? After all, how many English words contain *ga* that is pronounced with a [j] sound?

(1)   Konogoro no maagarin wa mae yori zutto tabe-
      rareru yoo ni narimashita nee.
      "Margarine these days has become much more palatable than before, hasn't it?"

Maakyuro マーキュロ ($<$*Mercuro*chrome)

Maakyuro is an abbreviation of *Ma⌐akyurokuro⌐omu*. Since the full form is almost too long in Japanese, the shorter form is preferred. *Maakyuro* is interchangeably used with *aka-chin,* from Japanese *a⌐ka* "red" and *chin*.

This *chin* is the same *chin* in the second half of *yoochin,* an addreviation of *yoˉodochiˉnki* (from German *Jodtinktur*) "iodine tincture."

maˉdamu-kiˉraa マダム・キラー (lit. madame killer)

English *lady-killer* came into Japanese and became *reˉdii-kiˉraa.* The Japanese have gone one step farther to coin another related word *madamu-kiraa,* lit. "madame killer," meaning "a man who is irresistibly attractive to married women." One could use *oˉkusama-goˉroshi,* which is a non-loan version of *madamu-kiraa,* but the latter is probably a little more common.

maˉfuraa マフラー (＜muffler)

Mafuraa means two things. First, it means "heavy neck scarf."
(1) Sono mafuraa atataka soo desu nee.
   "Doesn't your muffler look warm?"

Second, a *mafuraa* is a device for deadening the sound of an automobile or motorcycle engine.
(2) Kuruma no mafuraa ga dame ni natta no de, ya-kamashii.
   "My car is noisy because the muffler is not working well."

When used in the first sense above, *mafuraa* has no non-loan equivalent. In the second sense, *mafuraa* could be replaced by the non-loan *sho⌈oo⌉nki.*

ma⌈karoni-ue⌉sutan マカロニ・ウエスタン
(lit. macaroni western)

A made-in-Italy western is called "a spaghetti western" in the United States, but the Japanese word for it is *makaroni-uesutan,* allegedly coined by movie critic Nagaharu Yodogawa (Yoshizawa, p. 477). In English, *spaghetti* has three syllables. and *macaroni* four. In Japanese, on the other hand, *su⌈page⌉tti* has five syllables, *makaroni* four. Perhaps *makaroni* was adopted because of its relative brevity.

ma⌈nee-bi⌉ru マネー・ビル (lit. *money buil*ding)

In the early fifties, body building was introduced to Japan and became known as *bo⌈dii-bi⌉rudingu* or, more frequently, *bodii-biru* for short. Shortly thereafter, stock companies and banks started using a new pseudo-loan *manee-biru,* patterned after *bodii-biru,* to mean "money-making." Moneymaking has been called *rishoku* and can still be called that, but *manee-biru* sounds more modern and therefore more appealing.

ma⌈nha⌉nto マンハント (lit. manhunt)

English *manhunt* refers to an intensive search for a

criminal, suspect, escaped convict, etc. Japanese *manhan-to,* on the other hand, does not mean that at all. Rather it refers to the act of hunting for eligible men by women, in the same sense as the non-loan *o⌐toko-a⌐sari.*

For some reason, looking around for eligible women is never called **u⌐umanha⌐nto,* but rather *ga⌐aruha⌐nto* (lit. girlhunt).

manneri マンネリ (<*manneri*sm)

English *mannerism* in the sense of "marked adherence to a particular manner" has become *ma⌐nneri⌐zumu* in Japanese, which is very often shortened to *manneri.* In this particular sense, *manneri* is probably used much more often in Japanese than *mannerism* is in English. For example, in the following example, one would be unlikely to use *mannerism* in English.

(1) Kare no manga wa konogoro manneri-gimi de, sappari omoshiroku nai.

"His cartoons vary so little (lit. tend to show such mannerism) these days that they aren't much fun any more."

Ma⌐rukusu-bo⌐oi マルクス・ボーイ (lit. Marx boy)

This word is an early Showa coinage, probably dating back to the late 1920's, when Marxism was a fad among young Japanese intellectuals. *Marukusu-booi* was a derogatory term that referred to young men who were always carrying books on Marxism for show without a real understanding of it. Although the word is no longer in use, it is included here because of its historical significance.

ma⌐sshu-po⌐teto マッシュ・ポテト
(＜*mash*ed *potato*es)

Mashed potatoes are generally called *masshu-poteto*. Because of the lack of plurals in Japanese, *masshu-poteto* has no plural form, never becoming **ma⌐sshu-po⌐tetozu*. Also, the past participle ending, *-ed,* in *mashed* was dropped in the process of borrowing, thus yielding *masshu*. (Although the full form, *ma⌐sshuto-po⌐teto,* is listed in most dictionaries, my hunch is that it is not half as common as *masshu-poteto*.) This phenomenon is quite prevalent, however. Consider, for example, *koon-biifu* "*corn*ed *beef*," *kondensu-miruku* "*condense*d *milk*," and *sumooku-saamon* "*smoke*d *salmon*."

A well-educated Japanese man once told me that he used to believe until he was well into his fifties that *masshu* in *masshu-poteto* was originated from Japanese *mawashi* meaning "to stir, spin, or whirl [something]." Such false assumptions about loanwords are probably much more common than we might think.

ma¹suku マスク (＜mask)

Masuku has three main uses. First, it means a mask used in sports such as baseball, ice hockey, and diving. Second, it refers to cold weather masks made of gauze, which Japanese wear very frequently during the cold winter months. Third, it means "looks" or "facial features," especially with reference to actors.

(1) Ano haiyuu wa hori ga fukakute chotto gaijin-fuu no masuku o shite-iru.

"That actor has well-sculptured features, which make him look somewhat Caucasian."

This third use developed in Japanese independently of the original English word.

ma¹zaa-konpurek¹kusu マザー・コンプレックス
(＜mother complex)

Mazaa-konpurekkusu has a meaning similar to *Oedipus complex*. The word refers to the confused mental state of a son who, as a result of being raised indulgently by his mother, develops excessive psychological dependence on her, which affects his later relationships with other women. Since *mazaa-konpurekkusu* is a long word, it is often abbreviated as *maza-kon*.

(1) Ano otoko mazakon na no ka, kekkon-shita bakari na no ni oku-san to umaku itte-inai rashii.

"That guy must be suffering from a 'mother complex.' He got married just recently, but already it

looks as though he isn't getting along with his
wife."

In today's Japan, where the father is often a work-
aholic working for his company until late hours and even
on weekends, the mother frequently ends up directing
her entire attention and affection to her oldest son, thus
creating in him a *mazaa-konpurekkusu*. In a way, *mazaa-
konpurekkusu* may be called an inevitable outcome of
Japan's rapid growth in GNP.

me⌐eku-be⌐ddo　メーク・ベッド　(lit. make bed)

In English, *make a bed* means not only "to manufac-
ture a bed" but more frequently "to put a bed in the proper condition or state, as for use." There is no non-loan
in Japanese specifically indicating the latter meaning.
Hotels have started using *meeku-beddo* (lit. make bed)
and *be⌐ddo-me⌐ekingu* "bed-making" to refer to the act of
making a bed. What is interesting is the fact that the
article *a* in *make a bed* has been dropped in Japanese,
thus yielding *meeku-beddo* rather than **me⌐eku-a-be⌐ddo*.
Articles being left out is not an uncommon phenomenon
with loanwords, however. Other examples are *ofu-reko*
(<*off* the *reco*rd) and *o⌐n-e⌐a* (<*on* the *air*).

me⌐ekya⌐ppu　メーキャップ　(<make-up)

Meekyappu comes from English *make-up*, but it is used

only in the sense of "the application of cosmetics." Why *make-up* first became *meekyappu* in Japanese rather than *me⌈eku-a⌉ppu* is a mystery. Lately, however, this latter version, *meeku-appu,* has become popular also, and with a wider range of meaning as well. While *meekyappu* usually referred to the application of cosmetics by actors, *meeku-appu* seems to refer to the act of applying cosmetics by anyone. *Meeku-appu* may be shortened to *me⌈eku.*

(1) Hanako wa meeku o shinagara, kagami no naka no kao o nagameta.

"Hanako gazed at her face in the mirror as she put her make-up on."

Of course, the non-loan *ke⌈sho⌉o* (or *okeshoo*) would mean the same thing, and is still used more often than *meeku-appu,* but the latter's use is definitely spreading.

me⌈jaa-ka⌉ppu メジャー・カップ (lit. measure cup)

Mejaa-kappu means "measuring cup," but the *-ing* ending of *measuring* was obviously dropped in Japanese. The same is true of *measuring spoon,* which became *me⌈-jaa-supu⌉un* (lit. measure spoon) instead of **me⌈jaringu-supu⌉un.* The dropping of *-ing* is of course for the sake of brevity. Another example of this type is *ha⌈ppii-e⌉ndo* (lit. happy end), meaning "happy ending."

Mejaa-kappu is interchangeably used with *ke⌈iryoo-ka⌉ppu* (*keiryoo* of which is a non-loan meaning "measuring"), or simply shortened to *ka⌉ppu.*

me⌐nchi メンチ (lit. mince)

Menchi, or *mi⌐nchi,* comes from English *mince,* but is misapplied to mean "ground meat." Ground meat is usually called *hiki-niku,* a non-loan, in the Tokyo area, but in some other regions of Japan it is often called *menchi* or *minchi.*

Me⌐nchi-ka⌐tsu (lit. mince cutlet) is a kind of cutlet made from ground meat mixed with minced onions. It is cheaper than a regular cutlet and is therefore served at cheap eating places such as college cafeterias.

The fact *mince* became *menchi* rather than *⌐mi⌐nsu* indicates that the word was borrowed by ear quite some time ago, probably in early Meiji.

mini-komi ミニ・コミ (lit. *mini-commu*nication)

Mini-komi is a pseudo-loan created as an antithesis to *masu-komi,* a shorter version of *ma⌐su-komyunike⌐e-shon* "mass communication." *Mini-komi* refers to small-scale communication and to means used for that purpose, particularly such publications as company newsletters, citizens' campaign literature, etc. According to Yoshizawa and Ishiwata (p. 617), the word was coined about 1970.

It is interesting to note that while the word *masu-komi* was born as an abbreviation of the older and longer *masu-komyunikeeshon, mini-komi* was created as such from the very beginning. There is therefore no such form as *⌐mi⌐ni-komyunike⌐eshon.*

mi⌐ruku-ho⌐oru　ミルク・ホール　(lit. milk hall)

Miruku-hooru is a pseudo-loan coined, I suppose, after the pattern of *bi⌐a-ho⌐oru*. The logic behind *miruku-hooru* was probably something like "If a bar-like place that serves beer is a *bia-hooru,* a restaurant-like place that serves milk should be called a *miruku-hooru.*" *Miruku-hooru* existed from the Taisho period until early Showa. They served milk and other nonalcoholic beverages as well as light meals. If my memory is correct, they had almost completely been replaced by *kissaten* "coffee shops" by the time World War II started. Nowadays I would be surprised if there were even one *miruku-hooru* left in Japan.

mi⌐ruku-ko⌐ohii　ミルク・コーヒー　(lit. milk coffee)

Miruku-koohii is a pseudo-loan meaning "coffee with milk." It contrasts with *bu⌐rakku-ko⌐ohii,* which naturally comes from *black coffee.*

What complicates the matter is the presence of another pseudo-loan *ko⌐ohii-mi⌐ruku* (lit. coffee milk), which actually means milk with a little coffee mixed in. This is a drink usually sold in a bottle and is available at such places as concessions at railroad stations.

mi⌐ruku-suta⌐ndo　ミルク・スタンド　(lit. milk stand)

A stall for the sale of fruit is a fruit stand. Likewise,

in English, one may speak of a newsstand and a hotdog stand, but, for some reason, never of a *milk stand. *Miruku-sutando* is obviously a Japan-made word meaning "a stall where milk is served." A *miruku-sutando* is most often located at a railroad station for the use of commuters who need a quick pick-me-up.

(1) Miruku-sutando de gyuunyuu o ip-pon nonde kara, densha ni norimashoo.

    "Let's take the next train after a bottle of milk at the 'milk stand.'"

mi⌐sa⌐iru　ミサイル　(<missile)

In America, *missile* is pronounced [mísəl]. To pronounce it [mísail] would be considered British. For some reason, this latter pronunciation was introduced to Japan and became *misairu.* Sometimes the non-loan *yu⌐udooda⌐n* is used, but almost always as a written form. In speech, *misairu* is the norm.

The reason the American pronunciation was disregarded was, according to my conjecture, that the word *missile* was introduced as a written word, and not as a spoken word. Since a great number of English words ending in *-ile* (e.g. *file, smile,* and *crocodile*) are pronounced with [-ail], it is natural that Japanese first encountering the word *missile* thought [mísail] would be the only possible pronunciation. Hence *misairu.*

(1) Nihon ni misairu-kichi ga dono-gurai aru ka shitte-imasu ka.

"Do you know how many missile bases there are in Japan?"

misu ミス (<*mis*take)

Unlike English *miss,* Japanese *misu* means "error." It is quite likely, therefore, that *misu* does not come from *miss,* but rather from *mistake.*

(1) Taihen na misu o yatte-shimatta.
"I made a very serious mistake."

In informal speech, especially by young people, *misu* is probably used almost as commonly as non-loans such as *shippai.*

Misu is also used as a verb with the addition of *-suru,* as in

(2) Ikura Yoshida-san de mo, tama ni wa misu-suru koto mo arimasu yo.
"Even Mr. Yoshida could make an error once in a while, you know."

In highly idiomatic speech, *misu-suru* even becomes *misu-ru* and is inflected like any other *-u* verb.

(3) Kondo wa misu-ranai yoo ni shiyoo.
"I'll try not to make a mistake this time."

misupuri ミスプリ (<*mispri*nt)

Misupuri is often used as an abbreviation of the full form *misupurinto* "misprint."

(1)   Kono hon wa misupuri[nto] ga oo-sugiru.
       "This book has too many misprints."

Goshoku, a non-loan, is used just as frequently to mean the same thing.

mobi⌐reeji   モビレージ   (lit. auto *mobile* + vil *lage*)

Mobireeji is a new pseudo-loan meaning "campsite for automobile owners." In Japan, most campsites are barred to motor traffic. New campsites have been opened recently specifically designed for car owners, by the name of *mobireeji.* In America, since most campsites are open to automobiles, there is no need to coin a new word as there was in Japan. There is consequently no equivalent of *mobireeji* in English.

mobo   モボ   (< *mo*dern *bo*y)

Mobo is short for *mo⌐dan-bo⌐oi.* According to Yoshizawa (p. 586), the term *modan-booi* was originally coined about 1930 by Sōichi Ōya, a social critic, to refer to the frivolous and epicurian young men of that period, who most typically had a mustache, carried a cane, and wore bell bottoms. Since their looks and lifestyle were so different from what Japanese society had been used to until that time, a new name for this new breed was called for, which was provided by Ōya. Eventually *modan-booi* was shortened to *mobo,* which then became more common than the original full form.

mo⌐ga モガ (<*mo*dern *girl*)

Moga is an abbreviation of *mo⌐dan-ga⌐aru*. The etymology of *modan-gaaru* is not certain. According to Arakawa (p. 1374), the word was coined by Chōgo Usui, who wrote an essay "Modan-gaaru-ron ('On Modern Girls')" in *Josei* magazine in 1919 or 20. According to Yoshizawa (p. 586), however, Sōichi Ōya, who was the first to use the word *mo⌐dan-bo⌐oi* (see *mo⌐bo*), was also responsible for the creation of *modan-gaaru* about 1930. Be that as it may, *modan-gaaru* refers to the young girls of the 1920's who wore bobbed hair, high heels, and long skirts. In short, *modan-gaaru* were the Japanese counterpart of flappers.

According to Umegaki (1976b, p. 303), it was probably a newspaper editor who shortened *modan-gaaru* to *moga* for space-saving purposes. *Moga* soon came to be more commonly used than the full form.

mo⌐oningu-ka⌐ppu モーニング・カップ

(lit. morning cup)

Mooningu-kappu is a pseudo-loan literally meaning "morning cup." As coffee becomes increasingly popular in Japan, more and more people wish to drink not just a regular cup but a large cup of coffee for breakfast. *Mooningu-kappu* fulfill this need. They are very much like coffee mugs used in America but look different in shape.

They are shaped more like regular cups but are made larger.

(1) Asa mooningu-kappu de koohii o nonde kara kai-
     sha e dekakeru hito ga zuibun ooku natte-kita yoo
     desu.
     "It seems that the number of people who go to
     work after drinking a mug of coffee in the morning
     has increased quite a bit."

mooningu-kooru モーニング・コール
                                        (lit. morning call)

Suppose you are staying at a hotel and must get up early the next morning but do not have an alarm clock. You will naturally use the hotel's "mooningu-kooru" service by calling up the front desk, asking to be awakened at a designated hour. They will then call you in the morning to wake you up as requested. *Mooningu-kooru* refers both to this service and to the call they place.

mopaato モパート (lit. *mo*torcar + a*part*ment house)

Before World War II and shortly thereafter, only rich people living in ritzy houses could afford automobiles. Apartment house dwellers simply did not belong to this category. From the late '50s on, however, as Japan's economic growth continued, exclusive apartment houses by the name of *manshon* (lit. mansion) began to be built for well-to-do families who owned cars. To satisfy future tenants' need for garage spaces, some of these "manshon" had a garage underneath. Hence the name *mopaato* (lit. *mo*torcar + *apart*ment house). The first of this kind appeared in Meguro-ku, Tokyo, in 1959 (Jiyūkokuminsha, 1976, p. 988).

mu˥udii　ムーディー　(lit. moody)

Muudii comes from English *moody* but has an entirely different meaning. Apparently the individual who first started using the word did not know the meaning of the original English word.

In English, the word *mood* is neutral in meaning. It may have a positive or negative meaning, depending on the modifier, as in "He's in a bad mood" or "He's in a good mood." In Japanese, on the other hand, *mu˥udo* (from *mood*) generally has a nice connotation, as in *Asoko wa muudo no aru kissaten da,* which is literally "That's a coffee shop with a mood" but actually means "That's a coffee shop with a pleasant atmosphere." As indicated in my *English Loanwords in Japanese* (pp. 104-105), this is due to the fact that *muudo* came into Japanese via "mood music," the type of music suggesting a mood of languorous relaxation. Someone later started using *muudii* as an adjective form of *muudo* in such sentences as *Are wa muudii na merodii desu nee* (lit. Isn't that a moody melody?), which is supposed to mean "Isn't that a melody that creates a pleasant, languorous mood?" Unfortunately, however, English *moody* is used only in an unfavorable sense, i.e. "ill-humored" or "temperamental." If, therefore, a Japanese speaking English uses *moody* in the sense of Japanese *muudii,* he will be in deep trouble. Katō (pp. 78-79) writes about exactly such a person, a Japanese student in America who was invited to an American home and ended up baffling the whole family by calling their house a "moody" one!

naiibu ナイーブ (<naive)

English *naive* originally comes from French, but all loanword dictionaries I consulted ascribe Japanese *naiibu* to English *naive*; I shall therefore follow suit here.

Naiibu is different from *naive* in that the former always carries a laudatory connotation whereas the latter does not. In Japanese, *naiibu* means "innocent" or "unaffected," as in

(1)   Aayuu naiibu na seinen wa konogoro mezurashii.
      "It is so rare to find an innocent, unaffected young man like that these days."

In English, on the other hand, *naive* often means "lacking experience, judgment, or information," as in *He has a naive attitude toward communism.*

na⌐nbaa-pure⌐eto ナンバー・プレート

(lit. number plate)

License plates on cars, buses, motorcycles, etc., are called *nanbaa-pureeto,* not **ra⌐isensu-pure⌐eto.* Either *nanbaa-pureeto* comes from British *number plate,* or someone decided that it would be better to use the already familiar loanword *na⌐nbaa* instead of the still unfamiliar *ra⌐isensu.*

(1) Nihon de wa nanbaa-pureeto ga kuruma no zengo ni tsuite-iru.

"In Japan, cars carry license plates both in the front and on the back."

Incidentally, in the United States, where some states allow license plates with non-number identifications such as the owner's initials, *number plate* would indeed be an inaccurate appelation.

ne⌐eburu ネーブル （<*navel* orange）

In Japanese, the word for a navel is a non-loan, *heso* or *oheso.* A navel orange, however, is called *ne⌐eburu-o⌐renji,* which is often shortened to *neeburu.* Japanese speakers of English must never forget that, in English, a navel orange is always called a navel orange, and never just a navel.

(1) Kono neeburu o itsutsu kudasai.

"I'd like five of these navel oranges, please."

ne⌐ru ネル (<flan*nel*)

Neru is an abbreviation of *furanneru* "flannel" (see *furanneru*). According to Yoshizawa and Ishiwata (p. 413), *neru* is usually cotton flannel in Japan whereas *hon-neru* (*hon* being a non-loan meaning "genuine") refers to wool flannel.

The loanword *neru* has an accent on the first syllable and is therefore pronounced differently from the non-loan *neru*, a verb meaning "to sleep" or "to go to bed," which is accentless.

nonpori ノンポリ (<*nonpoli*tical)

During the '60s, when university campuses in Japan, exactly as in the United States, were in great turmoil, some students became radically political. There were, however, a great many students who remained completely apolitical. This latter category and the students who fell in this category were called *nonpori*.

(1) Ano hito wa gakusei-jidai zutto nonpori datta.
     "He was nonpolitical all through college."

no⌐n-se⌐kuto ノン・セクト (lit. non-sect)

Like *nonpori* (see *nonpori*) *non-sekuto* was also a product of the turbulent sixties. Unlike *nonpori* students, *non-sekuto* students were interested in campus politics, but they were dissatisfied with the existing factions among the student activists. They were the group of students who wanted to remain individuals by not getting involved in factional strife.

noo-bura ノー・ブラ (lit. no bra)

Noo-bura means "without a bra," as in

(1) Amerika de wa konogoro noo-bura ga hayatte-iru soo desu yo.
    "I hear it's getting quite common in the United States not to wear a bra."

noo-geemu ノー・ゲーム (lit. no game)

A baseball game called because of darkness, bad weather, etc., before the fifth inning is over is a *noo-geemu*. This word is probably used as frequently as the non-loan *mukoo-jiai* (lit. nullified game).

(1) Shiai wa nichibotsu no tame noo-geemu ni natta.
    "The game was called because of darkness."

Noo-geemu is not synonymous with *kooorudo-geemu* (see *koorudo-geemu*).

noo-katto ノー・カット (lit. no cut)

Movies that contain obscene scenes have to have those scenes cut by the agency concerned before release.

Movies that are too long are also cut to appropriate length. This act of cutting is *ka꜒tto,* and the absence of *katto* is called *noo-katto.* In English, one would probably say "uncut" or "uncut version."

(1) Watanabe-san, Amerika de noo-katto no *Diipu-Surooto* o mita-tte hontoo desu ka.

"Mr. Watanabe, is it true that you saw the uncut version of *Deep Throat* in America?"

no꜒o-kura꜒tchi   ノー・クラッチ   (lit. no clutch)

Noo-kuratchi is a pseudo-loan meaning "automatic transmission." *O꜒otomachikku-toransumi꜒sshon,* a direct transliteration of *automatic transmission,* is also used but it is too long and cumbersome to replace *noo-kuratchi* completely.

(1) Noo-kuratchi no kuruma wa futsuu no yori gasorin o kuu to iwarete-imasu.

"They say that cars with automatic transmission consume more gasoline than ordinary ones."

no꜒o-pan-ki꜒ssa   ノー・パン喫茶   (<*no pan*ty+Japanese *kissa*ten "coffee shop")

Noo-pan-kissa is a combination of *noo-pan* (short for *noo-pantii* "no panty") plus Japanese *kissa* (short for *kissaten* "coffee shop"). It refers to coffee shops with waitresses wearing no panties as a gimmick to attract male customers. Coffee shops of this type, though illegal, came into being in 1980 or 1981.

no͟o-ta͟imu ノー・タイム (lit. no time)

Noo-taimu is used in baseball and other sports to announce the end of a time-out.

no͟o-ta͟tchi ノー・タッチ (lit. no touch)

Noo-tatchi is first of all a baseball term, as in
(1) Kyatchaa ni-rui e nagemashita ga, noo-tatchi de rannaa seefu.

"The catcher throws the ball to second, but the runner is safe on a missed tag."

Noo-tatchi is also used figuratively to mean "having nothing to do with something."
(2) Shushoo wa kishakaiken de sono koto ni wa noo-tatchi datta.

"The prime minister did not even mention that matter at the press conference."
(3) Agunyuu no rai-nichi wa minkan no shootai de, seifu wa mattaku noo-tatchi datta.

"Agnew's visit to Japan was sponsored by a civilian group; the government had nothing to do with it."

o͞iru-sho͞kku　オイル・ショック　(lit. oil shock)

In October 1973, the Arab nations shook the whole world by radically increasing the price of oil, making it clear at the same time that they would continue to use oil as a weapon to strengthen their position in the world. Their new militant stance hit Japan especially hard since its domestic production of oil is practically nil. The fact that the event was referred to as *oiru-shokku* "oil shock" in Japan while it was called "oil crisis" in the United States shows how severely Japan was affected at the time.

o͞mu-ra͞isu　オム・ライス　(lit. *om*elet *rice*)

Omu-raisu might be called a Japanese-style Western dish or a Western-style Japanese dish. It is fried rice mixed with chopped onions, chopped meat, and tomato ketchup and wrapped in a paper-thin plain omelet. It is usually served with a small amount of ketchup on top. This food is not served at high-class Western-style restaurants but rather at eating places for common folk such as school cafeterias and department store dining rooms.

omuretsu　オムレツ　(<omelet)

According to Umegaki (1975b, p. 203), although English *omelet* comes from French *omelette,* Japanese *omuretsu* probably comes from the English version. As in the case of some other early loans such as *baketsu* "bucket" and *do͞onatsu* "doughnut," the word-ending *t* in *omelet* yielded *tsu* instead of *tto*. Even one omelet, therefore, is *omuretsu,* not **o͞mure͞tto.*

What an average Japanese visualizes upon hearing the word *omuretsu* is almost always one particular kind with ground beef and chopped onions inside, a popular Westernized dish.

o͞obaa-do͞kutaa   オーバー・ドクター

(lit. over-doctor)

Jiyūkokuminsha (1976, p. 1016) lists this new pseudo-loan, *oobaa-dokutaa,* as the equivalent of the non-loan *ha͞kushi-ro͞onin.* It refers to people who are "over" the doctorate stage (i. e. who have already completed the doctoral course work) but have no jobs.

o͞odaa-me͞edo   オーダー・メイド

(lit. order-made)

This pseudo-loan was coined as an antithesis to *re͞dii-me͞edo* "ready-made [clothes]." In normal English, one would say *custom-made.*

Oodaa-meedo is the equivalent of the non-loan *chu͞u-mo͞n-fuku* (lit. order [ed] clothes), but sounds more up-to-date.

o͡o-pea-ga͡aru　オー・ペア・ガール　(＜au pair girl)

Oo-pea-gaaru became popular in the mid-'70s. They are girls who go to England, live with host families, receive free room and board plus a small allowance in exchange for house work, and attend school during off-hours. According to Fukazawa (p. 266), there are three types of au pair girls: (1) those who have wanted to go abroad for a number of years and have already attained some proficiency in English, (2) those who have not studied English that seriously but now wish to learn to speak English before graduating from college, and (3) those who have hit a snag in their lives and are searching for a new direction. Fukazawa claims that this third group may very possibly reflect the closedness of Japanese society, which is particularly hard on young girls in rural areas.

Oo-pea-gaaru is sometimes shortened to *oo-pea* or simply *o-pea*. There is no non-loan counterpart.

o͡opun　オープン　(＜open)

The English adjective *open,* as the opposite of *closed,* usually corresponds to *aite-iru* in Japanese, as in
(1)　Mado ga aite-iru.
　　　"The window is open."
The use of *oopun* corresponding to the adjective *open* is reserved only for very special expressions such as *o͡opun-*

sute⌐eji "open, i.e. outdoor stage," *o⌐opun-go⌐rufu* "open golf tournament," and *o⌐opun-ka⌐raa* (lit. open collar, i.e. open-neck [sport] shirt).

Nowadays *oopun* corresponding to the verb *open* is commonly used to refer to the opening of a new business, especially in advertisements.

(2)   Rai-getsu tooka oopun!

"We are opening on the 10th of next month!"

Non-loans that used to be used with this meaning, such as *kaijoo, kaiten,* and *kaigyoo,* seem to appear less and less in advertisements although they are probably still the norm in speech.

The opening of a door, a window, etc., still requires a non-loan, *akeru.*

(3)   Atsui kara, mado o akemashoo.

"It's so hot! Let's open the windows."

In this case, *akeru* is never replaced by *oopun.*

o⌐oto-pa⌐araa　オート・パーラー　(lit. auto-parlor)

Ooto-paaraa is a new pseudo-loan meaning "automat," i.e. a restaurant using coin-operated equipment for dispensing food for customers. According to Sanseidō (p. 117), the first *ooto-paaraa* opened in Tokyo in 1962.

pa⌐in-ju⌐usu　パイン・ジュース　(<*pine*apple *juice*)

Pineapple juice is regularly called *pain-juusu* in Japa-

nese, and rarely *pa⌐inappuru-ju⌐usu* "pineapple juice."
Pineapple itself, however, is always *pa⌐ina⌐ppuru,* and
never **pa⌐in.*

(1) Painappuru wa Okinawa de takusan toremasu.
     "A lot of pineapples are grown in Okinawa."
(2) Kono pain-juusu wa tsumetakute oishii desu.
     "This pineapple juice is cold and tasty."

pa⌐ipu-ka⌐tto パイプ・カット (lit. pipe cut)

Paipu-katto is a crude way of referring to a contra-
ceptive operation for the male whereby the vas deferens
is tied with a piece of silk thread.

pa⌐kku パック (<pack, *pack*age)

English *pack* in the sense of "a pastelike cosmetic
material usually applied to the face" became *pakku* in
Japanese. There are different kinds such as *e⌐ggu-pa⌐kku*
"egg pack," *fu⌐ruutsu-pa⌐kku* "fruit pack," and *ho⌐rumon-
pa⌐kku* "hormon pack."

(1) Ano hito pakku de mo yatte-iru no kashira. Kono-
     goro zuibun kirei ni natta keredo.
     "I wonder if she is using a pack. She looks much
     more beautiful these days."

Pakku also means "package tour," as is the case
with *Ja⌐ru-pa⌐kku* "JAL PAK," i. e. package tours offered by Japan Airlines. Package tours used to be called

da⌐ntai-ryo⌐koo, a non-loan meaning "group tour," until 1965, when JAL started offering package tours by the name of *Jaru-pakku.*

(2) Jaru-pakku de Yooroppa e itte-kimashita.

"I took a JAL package tour to Europe."

pa⌐nchi パンチ (<punch)

Panchi, from English *punch,* has several meanings. First, it is a blow with the fist, especially in boxing.

(1) Joo Ruisu no panchi wa sugokatta nee.

"Joe Louis had a great punch, didn't he?"

Second, *panchi* is a tool or machine for punching holes in paper.

Third, *panchi* refers to a beverage consisting of spirits, lemon, sugar, spices, etc. It is not as common a party drink in Japan as it is in the United States. When used in this sense, *panchi* is sometimes pronounced *po⌐nchi* as well.

In Japan, there is a fruit dish very similar to a fruit cocktail, and it is called *fu⌐ruutsu-po⌐nchi,* which is literally "fruit punch" but isn't a drink. In the expression *furuutsu-ponchi, po⌐nchi* is for some reason never replaced by *panchi.*

(2) Kono kissaten no furuutsu-ponchi totemo oishii kara, tabete-mimasen ka?

"This coffee shop serves a terrific fruit cocktail. How about trying it?"

pan-suto　パンスト　(lit. *pan*ty *sto*cking)

　　Pan-suto is an abbreviation of *paˉntii-sutoˉkkingu* meaning "panty hose." Panty hose was first introduced to Japan in 1968 (Yoshizawa and Ishiwata, p. 468), about the time miniskirts became the fad. Panty hose, however, did not become **paˉntii-hoˉozu* in Japanese. The reason was probably because English *hose* was familiar to the Japanese only in the sense of "flexible tube for water," but not in the sense of "stocking." Therefore, the Japanese created a new pseudo-loan, *pantii-sutokkingu* (lit. panty stocking), from two loanwords that were already familiar to most Japanese: *paˉntii* "panty" and *suˉtoˉkkingu* "stocking." This practice of replacing part of an English compound with a familiar loan to create a new pseudo-loan is a fairly common one, as in the case of *guˉroobu-boˉkkusu* (lit. glove box) meaning "glove compartment" (see *guroobu-bokkusu*) or *naˉnbaa-pureˉeto* (lit. number plate) meaning "license plate" (see *nanbaa-pureeto*).

　　Don't confuse the shorter form, *pan-suto,* with *han-suto,* an abbreviation of *haˉngaa-sutoraˉiki* "hunger strike" (see *han-suto*).

peˉejento　ページェント　(<pageant)

　　Peejento, from English *pageant,* used to mean "outdoor [theatrical] play." Lately it has acquired a new meaning, i.e. "colorful procession."

English *pageant* may sometimes be pronounced [péijənt] in England, but even there that pronunciation does not seem to be as common as [pǽjənt], which, in the United States, is the only acceptable pronunciation. The fact that *pageant* became *peejento,* and not **pa⌉jento,* shows that the first part of *pageant* was probably mis-identified with *page,* which had already yielded *peeji* in Japanese.

pe⌈epaa-dora⌉ibaa　ペーパー・ドライバー
(lit. paper driver)

There are many owners of drivers' licenses in Japan who do not own cars and therefore do not have much opportunity to put their licenses to actual use. These people are called *peepaa-doraibaa* meaning "potential drivers who are temporarily enjoying only the possession of required papers, i. e. licenses."

(1) Nagai aida peepaa-doraibaa deshita ga, kondo
yatto kuruma o kaimashita yo.
"I've been a licensed driver without a car for a long time, but recently I've finally bought a car."

pe⌈epaa-te⌉suto　ペーパー・テスト　(lit. paper test)

A written exam is usually called a *hi⌈kki-shike⌉n,* a non-loan, but there is also a new pseudo-loan meaning the same thing, *peepaa-tesuto* (lit. paper test), so called because a written test is of course written on paper.

pe⌐epaa-tora⌐beraa   ペーパー・トラベラー
(lit. paper traveler)

Peepaa-toraberaa is a fairly new pseudo-loan referring to a person who has a passport (made of paper, of
course) but has neither taken a trip abroad nor has any
immediate plans for future trips. Of all the dictionaries
I consulted, only Jiyūkokuminsha (1976, p. 1278) had
this word listed, as compared with *pe⌐epaa-dora⌐ibaa,*
which is included in every one of them. Apparently
peepaa-toraberaa is not as common a word as *peepaa-
doraibaa.*

pe⌐nshon   ペンション   (<pension)

The Japanese equivalent of *pension* meaning "annuity
paid after retirement" is a non-loan, *onkyuu* or *nenkin.*
(1)   Ato juugo-nen shitara, onkyuu o moratte taishoku-
      suru tsumori desu.
      "In 15 more years, I'll be retiring on a pension."
The loanword *penshon* comes from *pension* in the
sense of "boarding house." Japanese *penshon* is used
with a very specialized meaning of "tourist home." When
used in the sense of "boarding house," English *pension*
is pronounced very much like the original French word,
i. e., [pansión]. Japanese *penshon* follows neither the

French nor the English pronunciation.

(2) Furansu e ittara, penshon ni tomaru to yasui desu
    yo.
    "When you go to France, stay at tourist homes.
    It'll be cheaper that way."

pi⌐inattsu-ba⌐taa　ピーナッツ・バター

(<peanut butter)

Peanut has been borrowed into Japanese as *pi⌐inat-
tsu,* not **pi⌐inatto. Peanut butter* is therefore *piinattsu-
bataa,* and never **pi⌐inatto-ba⌐taa.*

(1) Amerika no kodomo wa piinattsu-bataa to jamu
    no sandoitchi o yoku tabemasu ga, Nihon de wa
    piinattsu-bataa to jamu wa issho ni shimasen.
    "American children often eat peanut butter and
    jam sandwiches, but Japanese do not eat peanut
    butter and jam together."

pi⌐ke　ピケ　(<*picke*t)

English *picket* meaning "a person or a body of persons stationed before a business establishment, office
building, etc., to prevent workers from going in during
a strike" is a *pi⌐ke⌐tto* or simply *pike* in Japanese.

Picketing is *pi⌐ke⌐ttingu,* but this too is often shortened
to *pike.*

Picket line is *pi⌐ketto-ra⌐in, pi⌐ke-ra⌐in,* or simply *pike.*

Pike, therefore, can mean either "picket," "picketing," or "picket line."

(1)   Pike o yabutte naka ni hairu no wa muzukashii.
      "It is difficult to go through a picket line."

pi⌐npon   ピンポン   (<ping-pong)

Pinpon means "ping-pong," but there is a non-loan *takkyuu* (lit. table ball), which also refers to the same sport. According to Nishio (p. 170), *pinpon* is definitely preferred by old people, whereas young people use *takkyuu* almost exclusively. He also points out the fact that *pinpon* carries the connotation of a casual game available at a resort hotel or some such place whereas *takkyuu* recalls a more active sport varsity players might engage in.

pi⌐ru   ピル   (<pill)

Although a birth-control pill is often referred to as "the pill" in English, the word *pill* by itself may mean any kind of medicine in tablet form. In Japanese, on the other hand, *piru* almost always refers to birth-control pills. Other pills are called *joozai* "tablet-form medicine." There is a non-loan meaning "birth-control pill," i. e. *keikoo-hinin'yaku,* but *piru* is much simpler to say and write.

pi¹za ピザ (＜pizza)

Pizza is of course an Italian word, but the food pizza was introduced to Japan by American chains such as Shakey's. Most Japanese therefore thought *pizza* was an English word and pronounced it like one, i. e. *piza.* Others who know that *pizza* is pronounced like an Italian word even in America prefer the version *pi¹ttsa,* which, however, is not used as extensively as *piza.*

(1) Nihon de mo konogoro piza ga hayatte-kimashita ga, gaijin wa Nihon no piza wa oishikunai to ii-masu.

"Pizza has become very popular in Japan, too, but foreigners say that Japanese pizza does not taste very good."

There is no non-loan equivalent of *piza* or *pittsa.*

pi¹za-ha¹usu ピザ・ハウス (lit. pizza house)

A restaurant specializing in pizzas is called a *piza-hausu* in Japan, whereas, in America, a pizza restaurant is known as a pizzeria. Although a particular pizza restaurant or a perticular pizza restaurant chain might call itself "Pizza House" in America, this is different from Japanese *piza-hausu,* which is a generic term.

(1) Kyoo wa ano piza-hausu ni haitte-mimashoo ka.

"Shall we try that pizzeria today?"

pi⌐za-pa⌐i ピザ・パイ (<pizza pie)

Yoshizawa and Ishiwata as well as Sanseidō claim that *piza-pai* (or *pi⌐ttsa-pa⌐i*) was coined in Japan by putting *pi⌐za/pi⌐ttsa* and *pa⌐i* "pie" together. This is, however, incorrect. Americans occasionally say *pizza pie* instead of *pizza* alone, and this American usage, I am sure, was introduced to Japan, yielding *piza-pai* (or *pittsa-pai*).

purachina プラチナ (<platinum?)

English *platinum* should have yielded **purachinamu* in Japanese, but, according to Yokoi (p. 84), when the word was introduced in speech, Japanese did not hear the word-final consonant, *m,* and therefore created *purachina* instead. My conjecture, however, is that *purachina* may very well have come from another language, e. g. Dutch, which calls the element *platina* instead of *platinum.*

Purachina is used interchangeably with *hakkin* (lit. white gold), a non-loan referring to the same thing.

pu⌐ra-ho⌐bii プラ・ホビー (lit. *pla*stic *hobby*)

Pura-hobii is a pseudo-loan referring to the hobby of building plastic models of automobiles, airplanes, etc.
(1) Suzuki-san wa otona no kuse ni uchi de wa pura-hobii ni muchuu ni natte-iru soo desu.

"Despite the fact that he's an adult, Mr. Suzuki, I hear, is always busy at home building plastic models."

pu⌐rasu-a⌐rufa   プラス・アルファ   (lit. plus alpha)

Purasu-arufa comes from *plus x* in the sense of "plus something." The expression is often used in union wage negotiations. *Go⌐juuma⌐n-en pu⌐rasu-a⌐rufa,* for example, means "500,000 yen plus something," i. e. "500,000 yen plus an indefinite amount to be determined at the management's discretion."

The reason *plus x* became *purasu-arufa* instead of **pu⌐rasu-e⌐kkusu* "plus x" is that *x* written cursively looks very much like the Greek letter α, i.e. "alpha"!

pu⌐resu-ha⌐mu   プレス・ハム   (<*press*ed *ham*)

Puresu-hamu (lit. press ham) comes from *pressed ham,* of which the *-ed* ending was apparently dropped in the process of borrowing. Hence *puresu-hamu* rather than **pu⌐resuto-ha⌐mu. Puresu-hamu,* sometimes called *yose-hamu* (*yose* is a non-loan meaning "put things together"), is a rather cheap kind of ham made by pressing different kinds of meat together.

pu⌐sshu⌐-hon   プッシュ・ホン   (lit. push phone)

As is the case in the United States, dial telephones

are gradually being replaced in Japan by push-button-type telephones. These now telephones are called Touch-Tone telephones in America, but they are known as *pusshu-hon* in Japan. There is no non-loan equivalent.

(1) Kondo uchi no denwa mo pusshu-hon ni shima-shita.

"We've changed our phone to Touch-Tone recently."

ra¬beru　ラベル　(＜label)

Labels on bottles, jars, cans, etc., are *raberu,* which comes from English *label,* although an older form *retteru,* derived from Dutch *letter,* is also used to refer to the same object.

(1) Kono kusuri wa raberu o yoku yonde kara nonde-kudasai.

"Please take this medicine after reading the label carefully."

Raberu also refers to the label at the center of a phonograph record. In this case, *retteru* is never used.

(2) Rekoodo no raberu o yomeba, dare ga utatte-iru ka wakarimasu yo.

"If you read the label on the record, you'll know who's singing."

Raberu has another version, *re¬eberu,* which is closer to the original English pronunciation but not used as often. *Raberu* is an example of spelling pronunciation.

Other examples of spelling pronunciation are *ra͞jio*
"radio" (instead of **re͞ejio* or **re͞edio*), *airon* "iron (used
for pressing clothes)" (instead of *aian), *bu͞zaa* "buzzer"
(instead of **ba͞zaa*), etc.

ra͞ibu-ha͞usu ライブ・ハウス (lit. live house)

Raibu-hausu is a coffee shop or a snack bar with
live music provided by a jazz or rock band.

ra͞in-da͞nsu ライン・ダンス (lit. line dance)

Chorus girls at Radio City Music Hall in New York
are known for their chorus line or kick line, i. e. the
routine in which they line up sideways facing the audi-
ence and kick up their heels in unison. There are chorus
girls in Japan who do the same routine, and the dance
they perform as they line up laterally is called *rain-dansu,*
a pseudo-loan; the dancers who regularly do this routine
are known as *ra͞in-da͞nsaa* (lit. line dancer).

There used to be two famous groups of *rain-dansaa*
in Tokyo, one at Nihon Gekijo in the Yurakucho area
and one at Kokusai Gekijo in the Asakusa area. Now
that both of them are gone much to the regret of old-
timers, however, no *rain-dansu* can be seen on a regular
basis, as far as I know.

ra⌐ito⌐-ban ライト・バン (lit. light van)

Raito-ban is a pseudo-loan that refers to a kind of van—a very small truck with a door in the back for loading and unloading.

(1) Raito-ban ga tsukaeru to hikkoshi ni benri na n desu ga nee.

"Wouldn't it be convenient for moving if we could use a small van?"

ra⌐n-endo-hi⌐tto ラン・エンド・ヒット

(lit. run-and-hit)

Hani (p. 36) points out that, in Japanese baseball terminology, *ran-endo-hitto* is sometimes mistakenly used instead of *hi⌐tto-endo-ra⌐n* to mean "hit-and-run." Of course, in American baseball, *hit-and-run* is never replaced by **run-and-hit*. *Ran-endo-hitto* was probably coined by some know-it-all who thought it would be more descriptive than *hitto-endo-ran* because in a hit-and-run play, the runner always starts running before the batter hits the ball!   (Also see *e⌐ndo⌐-ran.*)

ra⌐nningu-ho⌐omaa ランニング・ホーマー

(lit. running homer)

In Japanese baseball, an inside-the-park homerun is known as a *ranningu-hoomaa,* a pseudo-loan. An inside-the-park homerun is of course not the kind that is hit into the outfield bleachers, but the kind that the batter must earn by running hard. In that sense, as Hani (p. 45) points out, this pseudo-loan is more vividly descriptive and more to the point than the original English term and may be called a well-made pseudo-loan.

There are other baseball terms coined in Japan that are just as well-made. One example of these would be *sa⌐yonara-hoomu⌐ran,* a half-Japanese and half-loan term meaning "game-ending homerun."

re⌐beru-a⌐ppu レベル・アップ (lit. level up)

Reberu-appu is one of those pseudo-loans made up of a noun plus *a⌐ppu* "up." Other examples of this type are *imeeji-a⌐ppu* (lit. image-up) meaning "improving one's image," *be⌐esu-a⌐ppu* (lit. base-up) meaning "increase in base pay," and *ko⌐suto-a⌐ppu* (lit. cost-up) meaning "increase in cost."

Reberu-appu is used with the non-loan *suru* "to do" to mean "to raise the level/standard of something," as in

(1) Nihon no yakyuu wa mukashi to kuraberu to daibu reberu-appu-shita yoo da.

"It seems that the level of Japanese baseball has risen higher than where it used to be."

Instead of *reberu-appu,* one can easily use non-loans to mean the same thing, e.g. *suijun o ageru* "to raise the standard of something" and *suijun ga agaru* "The stan-

dard of something rises." Many people, especially jour-
nalists, however, often prefer *reberu-appu* for two reasons.
First, *reberu-appu* is a newer word and sounds more up-
to-date than its non-loan equivalents. Second, it is easier
to write *reberu-appu* in katakana, i.e. レベル・アップ,
than to write *suijun o ageru* in kanji and hiragana, i.e.
水準を上げる.

re⌐beru-da⌐un   レベル・ダウン   (lit. level-down)

Reberu-daun is the opposite of *re⌐beru-a⌐ppu* (see *reberu-appu*) and means "lowering the level/standard of
something."

(1)   Nihon no suiei wa konogoro reberu-daun desu nee.
      "Japanese swimming has gone downhill in recent
      years, hasn't it?"

As is the case with *reberu-appu, reberu-daun* is more
up-to-date, more journalistic, and easier to write than its
non-loan equivalents, i.e. *suijun o sageru* "to lower the
standard of something" and *suijun ga sagaru* "The standard of something goes down."

re⌐jidensu   レジデンス   (<residence)

Modern, high-class apartment houses and condomin-
iums are known as *ma⌐nshon* (lit. mansion) in contrast
with *a⌐pa⌐ato,* which refers to more reasonably-priced,
and less fancy apartment houses. Individual *manshon*

are usually given names from European languages, especially English, e.g. X Haitsu "X Heights," Y Hausu "Y House," and Z Koopo "Z Co-op." *Rejidensu* is just another word from English that is given to *manshon.*

(1) Tanaka-san wa Shibuya Rejidensu to yuu manshon ni sunde-iru soo desu.

"I hear Mr. Tanaka lives in a nice apartment house called Shibuya Residence."

re̍kkaa　レッカー　(<wrecker)

Rekkaa, from English *wrecker,* represents only one of the meanings of the latter, i.e. "tow truck."

(1) Kuruma ga ugokanaku nattara, rekkaa o tanomu yori shikata ga nai.

"When your car breaks down, the only thing you can do is to call a wrecker."

For some reason, neither *tow car* nor *tow truck* has been borrowed into Japanese.

re̍shiꟾibu　レシーブ　(<receive)

Japanese words for *receive* are almost always non-loans such as *uketoru,* as in

(1) Kesa Itoo-san kara tegami o uketorimashita.

"This morning, I received a letter from Mr. Ito."

The loanword *reshiibu* is used with a very specialized meaning, i.e. "receiving a serve (in such sports as tennis, ping-pong, and volleyball)."

(2) Saabu to reshiibu to dotchi ga muzukashii deshoo
     ka.
     "I wonder which is more difficult, to serve or to
     receive."

re⌐sutoran-shi⌐ataa レストラン・シアター
                                        (lit. restaurant theater)

A dinner theater is called *resutoran-shiataa,* a hybrid
pseudo-loan. *Re⌐sutoran* comes from French *restaurant,*
and *shi⌐ataa* from English *theater.*
(1) Resutoran-shiataa wa omoshiroi kedo, taka-sugi-
     masu yo.
     "Going to a dinner theater is fun but unfortunately
     costs too much."

re⌐taa-pe⌐epaa レター・ペーパー (lit. letter paper)

In America, paper used for letter writing is called
"stationery," "note paper," or "writing paper," none of
which has been borrowed into Japanese. *Retaa-peepaa*
(lit. letter paper) seems to come from British English.
    According to Nishio (p. 179) *retaa-peepaa* was once
a very common loanword, but is now dying out, almost
completely replaced by the non-loan *binsen.* In fact, this
is one of the very few cases where loanwords are gradually pushed over by their non-loan counterparts. Usually it is the other way around.

ri˥bingu-ki˥tchin　リビング・キッチン
(lit. *living* room + *kitchin*)

This is a pseudo-loan referring to a room which is a combination living room and kitchen. It became popular in the '60s. In writing, it is usually shortened to LK, pronounced e˥ru-ke˥e.

Ri˥izento-suta˥iru　リーゼント・スタイル
(<Regent style)

Remember the greasy hair style of Elvis Presley when he was young? He had his hair high in the front and combed back on either side. That was *Riizento-sutairu,* or *Ri˥izento* for short.

According to Yoshizawa (p. 137), the name *Regent* originates from London's Regent Street, where this particular hair style was the fad at one time. In Japan, this hair style was fairly popular shortly after World War II.

ri˥ko˥oru　リコール　(<recall)

Rikooru, from English *recall,* is usually used in one sense only, i. e. "the removal of a public official from office by a vote of the people." This right was given to the Japanese for the first time after World War II. They went one step farther than the Americans, i. e., they can recall even Supreme Court judges, although this has never happened yet in practice.

ri⌐suningu-ru⌐umu リスニング・ルーム

(<listening room)

Risuningu-ruumu usually refers to a room in a music store specially designed for listening to a stereo set.

ri⌐suto-a⌐ppu リスト・アップ (lit. list up)

Risuto-appu is regularly used with *suru* "to do" these days to mean "to make a complete list."

In English, *up* sometimes indicates completion, as in *eat up, drink up,* and *finish up.* It must have been someone with this knowledge who coined the new pseudo-loan, *risuto-appu.*

(1) Kono natsu-yasumi ni yomi-tai hon o risuto-appu-shite-mimashita.

"I've made a list of books I'd like to read during summer vacation."

ro⌐ke ロケ (<*loca*tion)

Roke is short for *ro⌐ke⌐eshon* "location," a movie term meaning "a place, outside of the studio, affording a suitable environment for filming a particular movie or scene."

(1) Konogoro wa Nihon-eega mo kaigai-roke de tsukuru koto ga ooku natte-kita.

"These days more and more Japanese movies are filmed on location overseas."

There is a non-loan counterpart, ya⌐gai-sa⌐tsuei (lit. outdoor filming), but it is not used as frequently as *roke* or *rokeeshon.*

According to Yoshizawa and Ishiwata (p. 709), it was in 1909 that a Japanese film was shot on location for the first time.

All other meanings of English *location* correspond to non-loans in Japanese.

ro⌐okaru ローカル (<local)

Although Japanese *rookaru* comes from English *local,* the two have two different meanings. In English, *local* usually means "pertaining to, characteristic of, or restricted to a particular place," as in *local custom, local news,* and *local government.* On the other hand, *rookaru* means "provincial" or "rural." In America, a TV station in New York that is not part of a national network is a "local" station. In Japanese, on the other hand, a TV station in Tokyo that is not part of a national network cannot be called *rookaru* since it is neither provincial nor rural. In other words, *rookaru* connotes "far from big cities like Tokyo."

Rookaru is used mostly in compounds, e. g. ro⌐okaru-ba⌐ngumi (lit. local [TV or radio] program), ro⌐okaru-nyu⌐usu (lit. local news), and ro⌐okaru-ho⌐osoo (lit. local broadcast or telecast). The difference between these Japanese compounds and their English counterparts is that the Japanese words strongly connote that these items cater to people living in the provinces.

ro͞on   ローン (<loan)

Roon, from English *loan,* has only one meaning, i. e. "a sum of money lent at interest by money-lending organizations such as banks." Although there is a non-loan which means the same thing, i. e. *kashitsukekin,* the loan-word *roon* is becoming increasingly more popular because it is easy to say and easy to write. *Roon* is often used in compounds such as *kaꞌa-roꞋon* (lit. car loan), *hoꞋomu-roꞋon* "home loan," and *kyoꞋoiku-roꞋon* (i. e. non-loan *kyooiku* "education" + *roon*).

(1) Uchi o tateru koto ni shita n desu ga, ginkoo kara dono-gurai hoomu-roon ga karirareru ka, mada wakarimasen.

"I've decided to build a house, but I don't know yet how big a home loan I can take out from my bank."

Some Japanese scholars seem to think that words such as *oꞋoto-roꞋon* "auto loan" and *hoꞋomu-roꞋon* "home loan" are pseudo-loans (e. g. Kashima, p. 44), but they are wrong. "Auto loan," "home loan," etc., are very commonly used in the United States.

roꞋosu   ロース (<roast)

Roosu, from English *roast,* came into Japanese probably in the early Meiji period. The fact that it is pronounced *roosu* instead of *ro͞osuto* shows that it was borrowed through the ear like some other early-Meiji loans such as *hankechi* "handkerchief," *shi͞chu͞u* "stew," and *kya͞betsu* "cabbage."

Roosu or *ro͞osu͞-niku* (*ni͞ku͞* being a non-loan meaning "meat") means "raw meat suitable for a roast." It is a kind of quality meat, expensive and tender, usually from the shoulder area of a cow, steer, or bull. Although *roosu* derives from *roast,* it is not always roasted. In fact, it is usually sold in slices, which Japanese may cook in any way they like. *Roosu* is usually beef, but the word also applies to other meats, particularly pork.

ro͞osu-ha͞mu   ロース・ハム   (lit. roast ham)

Roosu-hamu is quality ham. It is ham made from the kind of pork referred to as *ro͞osu* (see *roosu*) in Japanese. Most Japanese do not realize that there is no such English expression as *roast ham.

ro͞osuto   ロースト   (＜roast)

When meat is roasted, it is no longer *ro͞osu* (see *roosu*) but *roosuto.* In other words, *roosu* and *roosuto,* both of which come from the same English word *roast,* mean two different things. *Roosu* is a kind of quality meat still uncooked, whereas *roosuto* refers to already roasted meat.

Roosuto is usually used in compounds such as *ro⌐o-suto-biˉifu* "roast beef," *ro⌐osuto-chiˉkin* "roast chicken," and *ro⌐osuto-poˉoku* "roast pork."

(1) Kyoo no roosuto-biifu wa roosu-niku datta kara oishii deshoo.

"Today's roast beef is quality meat, so doesn't it taste good?"

ro⌐o-tiˉin   ロー・ティーン   (lit. low teen)

Youngsters about 13 or 14 are called *roo-tiin*. In English, however, one would probably say *early teens* rather than *low teens*.

(1) Roo-tiin no koro to iu no wa muzukashii jiki desu nee.

"The early teens are a difficult period, aren't they?"

The opposite is *ha⌐i-tiˉin* (lit. high teen), which would most likely be *upper teens* or *late teens* in English.

(2) Hai-tiin to iu no wa juushichi, juuhachi, juuku-gurai no wakamono no koto deshoo?

"By 'upper teens' don't they mean youngsters who are about 17, 18, or 19?"

ruˉbi   ルビ   (<ruby)

Rubi is a printing term that refers to small *kana* printed to the right of a Chinese character to show its pronunciation.

(1) Kono hon wa zenzen rubi ga futte (*or* tsukete) nai

kara, wakai hito ni wa yomi-nikui ka mo shire-masen.

"Because this book uses no *kana* alongside Chinese characters, it might be difficult for young people to read."

Rubi comes from English *ruby,* which, in Great Britain, refers to a 5 1/2-point type. In Japan, type used for *kana* showing the pronunciation of a Chinese character happened to be the same size as ruby type. Hence the name *rubi.*

The jewel *ruby,* however, is not *rubi* but *rubii* in Japan. This is one of those cases where the same English word has yielded two or more versions with different meanings in Japanese. Another example of this type would be *chalk,* which has yielded both *chako* (see *chako*) and *chooku.*

ruumu-chaaji ルーム・チャージ (lit. room charge)

A fee charged for a hotel room is called *ruumu-chaaji.* There is no corresponding English word.

saabu サーブ (<serve)

As is the case with *reshiibu* "receive" (see *reshiibu*), *saabu* is strictly a sports term used in such sports as tennis, ping-pong, volleyball, and badminton.

(1) Nan-nen tenisu o shite-ite mo, saabu ga heta ja dame da.

"No matter how many years you may have been
playing tennis, you're no good as long as you can't
serve well."

sa⌐afin サーフィン (<*surfing*)

Saafin is a new sport in Japan. It was virtually
unkown in Japan until the mid-'60s.

While most recent loanwords have been borrowed as
written words, *saafin,* despite its very recent origin, is a
hearing-based loan. Otherwise it would have become
**sa⌐afingu.* The names of other sports in English ending
in -*ing* have all become -*ingu* words in Japanese, e.g. *jo⌐-
gingu* "jogging," *ranningu* "running," *re⌐suringu* "wrestling," *fe⌐nshingu* "fencing," and *bo⌐kushingu* "boxing."
(1) Ichi-do Hawai de saafin o yatte-mitai to omotte-
     imasu.
     "I'd like to try surfing in Hawaii once."

sa⌐aji サージ (<serge)

Saaji comes from English *serge* meaning "twilled
fabric." *Serge* yielded another loanword *se⌐ru,* which is
used differently from *saaji* in that *seru* is restricted to
Japanese-style clothing, and *saaji* to Western-style clothing. (See *seru.*)
(1) Mukashi no gakusei wa minna saaji no seifuku o
     kite-ita mono datta.

"Formerly, students used to wear serge uniforms."

sa˺doru　サド ル　(<saddle)

A saddle for a horse is always *kura,* a non-loan. A
bicycle (or motorcycle) saddle, however, is called *sadoru.*
(1) Jitensha no sadoru ga chotto taka-sugiru kara,
hikuku-shite-kudasai.

"The saddle of my bicycle is a bit too high. Will
you lower it, please?"

There is no non-loan equivalent.

sa˺ido-bure˺eki　サイド・ブレーキ　(lit. side brake)

In Japanese, a hand brake could be called a *ha˺ndo-
bure˺eki* "hand brake," but probably more often it is
referred to as a *saido-bureeki,* a pseudo-loan.
(1) Chuusha-shitara kanarazu saido-bureeki o kakete-
kudasai.

"Please don't forget to pull the hand brake when
you park."

sa˺ido-te˺eburu　サイド・テーブル　(lit. side table)

Saido-teeburu sounds as though it was derived from
English *side table,* but these two words refer to two different types of furniture. In English, a side table is a
table intended to be placed against a wall, while a Jap-

anese *saido-teeburu* is a bed *side table* (Sanseidō, p. 256).

saⁱkuringu サイクリング (<cycling)

Americans do not use the word *cycling* very often. They seem to prefer words such as *bicycling* and *bicycle trip* instead. In Japanese, on the other hand, *saikuringu* in the sense of "bicycle trip" is used quite often, probably just as often as the non-loan equivalent *jiⁱtensha-ryoⁱkoo* "bicycle trip."

(1) Kondo mata doko ka e saikuringu ni ikimasen ka.
    "How about going on a bicycle trip again one of these days?"

saⁱrento サイレント (<silent)

Sairento, from English *silent*, has only one specialized meaning. It is short for *saⁱrento-eⁱiga* meaning "silent film."

(1) Eiga wa senkyuuhyakunijuu-nen-dai ni wa sairento ga daibubun datta.
    "Through the 1920's, most movies were silent."

Sairento-eiga can also be called *muⁱsei-eⁱiga* (lit. voiceless movie), a non-loan.

All other meanings of *silent* correspond to non-loans in Japanese, as in

(2) Suzuki-san wa kyoo wa fushigi ni nani mo iwanai nee.

"Mr. Suzuki is strangely silent today, isn't he?"

sa⌐maatai᠇mu   サマータイム   (lit. summertime)

Samaataimu or *sa⌐nmaata᠇imu* does not really mean "summer season." Instead, it means "daylight-saving time." The reason *daylight-saving time* became *samaataimu* in Japan is that * *de⌐eraito-seebingu-ta᠇imu* would have been impossibly long and unmanageable; besides, the British say *summertime* to mean "daylight-saving time," anyhow.

Samaataimu was first introduced to Japan in 1948 but was so unpopular that it was finally discontinued in 1952. To understand why it was so unpopular, one must go back to the time when it was introduced. It was still shortly after World War II, Japan had not made an economic recovery, and there was a constant food shortage. With *samaataimu,* evenings were so long that people became hungry again before going to bed and longed even more intensely for non-existing food. Furthermore, the Japanese at that time could not afford various forms of leisure-time activities such as golf and pleasure driving. Instead of using the saved daylight time for recreation, therefore, they just ended up working longer, getting less sleep at night and waking up more fatigued than ever. In other words, daylight-saving time is basically for the haves, and the Japanese, who were have-nots at the time, were not ready for it. Since it proved to be such a traumatic experience, even now, with a much higher standard of living, the Japanese are not likely to reintroduce *samaataimu,* at least in the foreseeable future.

Samaataimu has a non-loan equivalent, *na⌐tsuji⌐kan,* which is probably not used as often, at least, in conversation.

sa⌐rada   サラダ (<salad)

English *salad* is *sarada* in Japanese. English words ending in *-d* usually acquire the final syllable *do* when borrowed into Japanese, as in *be⌐ddo* "bed," *hu⌐udo* "hood," *ri⌐ido* "lead," etc. In fact, *sarada* may be the only *-da*-ending loan derived from a *-d*-ending English word. Arakawa (p. 496) shows with some examples that the version *sa⌐rado* existed in the beginning. The last example of *sarado* cited by him is as recent as 1925. *Sarado* was apparently gradually replaced by *sarada,* which is now the only possible version. The reason the final syllable changed from *do* to *da* was, as Ichikawa (p. 199) suggests, that the vowel in the first two syllables of *sarado* affected the word-final vowel. This is what he calls "a sort of vowel-harmony." (ibid.)

There is no non-loan equivalent of *sarada.*

sa⌐supe⌐ndaa   サスペンダー (<*suspender*s)

Sasupendaa brings back old memories. It means

"sock suspender[s]." Sock suspenders were used by men until the mid 1940's. After World War II, the idea of weaving elastic right into socks themselves was introduced from the United States, thus chasing *sasupendaa* completely out of the picture. *Sasupendaa* had a non-loan counterpart *ku⌐tsushita⌐dome,* which was used about as often.

Sasupendaa nowadays is used in the sense of "suspenders for trousers." It is probably used interchangeably with *zu⌐bo⌐ntsuri* (*zu⌐bo⌐n,* from French *jupon,* "trousers" +non-loan *tsuri* "suspend").

Like other loanwords such as *su⌐to⌐kkingu* "stocking[s]" and *su⌐ri⌐ppa* "slipper[s]," *sasupendaa* came into Japanese in the singular.

sasu-puro   サス・プロ   (<*su*staining *pro*gram)

Sasu-puro is an abbreviation of *sa⌐suteeningu-puro⌐-guramu,* meaning "radio or TV programs that are self-sustaining, i. e. programs financed by the radio or TV stations concerned without commercial sponsors." Since *sasuteeningu-puroguramu* is twelve syllables long, it is only natural that many people prefer the shorter *sasu-puro,* which has only four syllables.

There is a non-loan equivalent *ji⌐shuba⌐ngumi,* which is perhaps used as often.

se⌝ebu   セーブ   (<save)

Seebu is only used as a verb with the addition of *suru,* but its meaning is more limited than the original English word. *Se⌝ebu-suru* usually means "to hold back on something." For example, a baseball catcher might say to the pitcher:

(1) Mada ik-kai da kara, chikara o seebu-shita hoo ga ii yo.
     "It's only the first inning. You'd better save your strength."

Save as in *to save money,* however, corresponds to a non-loan such as *tameru* "to save" or *chokin-suru* "to save money."

(1) Mai-tsuki sukoshi-zutsu | okane o tamete-imasu.
                             | chokin-shite-imasu.
     "I save a little money each month."

Oka⌐ne o se⌝ebu-suru (lit. to save money) is not a normal sentence, if not completely wrong.

se⌐kando-ha⌝usu   セカンド・ハウス   (<second house)

Sekando-hausu comes from English *second house* but is used in the sense of "summer house," "weekend house," or "cottage." There is a non-loan equivalent *be⌝sso⌐o⌝,* but *sekando-hausu* sounds more up-to-date and therefore more desirable.

(1) Tonari no uchi ja kondo Karuizawa ni sekando-hausu o tateta n datte sa.

"You know something? I hear our next-door neighbor has just built a summer house in Karuizawa."

se̅kkusu セックス (＜sex)

Japanese *sekkusu* is much more limited in meaning than English *sex*. The fact of being either male or female is not referred to as *sekkusu,* but as *se̅i,* a non-loan. *Sekkusu* means either "sex organ," "sexual appetite," or, more frequently, "sexual intercourse." The non-loan *suru* "to do" is added to form *se̅kkusu-suru* "to have sex." There are some non-loans that refer to sexual intercourse such as *seikoo* or *se̅iko̅oi,* but these terms are all bookish whereas *sekkusu-suru* is more colloquial and more to the point.

Using a loanword often makes it easier for Japanese speakers to refer to taboo subjects. *Sekkusu-suru* is a good example of this. Other loanwords of this type are *to̅ire* "toilet" and *ma̅su* "masterbation."

sekohan セコハン (＜*seco*nd *han*d)

Secondhand in the sense of "previously used or owned," as in *secondhand clothes,* came into Japanese and took many forms (i.e. *se̅kandoha̅ndo, se̅kondohan̅do, sekohan, seko,* and *sekoo*), of which *sekohan* is probably the most common. There are some non-loans meaning the same thing, e.g. *chuuburu, chuuko,* etc., but whether they are loanwords or non-loans, all these words sound more derogatory in Japanese than their English counterparts (e.g. *secondhand* and *used*) do in English. The reason is that Japanese consumers strongly prefer brandnew items to used ones. In Japan, there is, for instance, no tradition of garage sales, which are very common in the United States. Foreign visitors to Japan are often astounded to find still fairly new and completely usable electric appliances discarded by the streetside.

se̚kusutashii　セクスタシー　(<*sex*+ecs*tasy*)

Sekusutashii was coined about 1956 (Jiyūkokumin-sha, 1976, p. 982) from two older loanwords, *se̚kkusu* "sex" and *e̚kusutashii* "ecstasy," to mean "sexual ecstasy." It was popular for a while, but like many other slang expressions, it too has become almost completely obsolete.

se̚rori　セロリ　(<celery)

The fact that *celery* yielded *serori* in Japanese indicates that it was introduced through the ear rather than through the eye. There were other variants at first, e. g. *she̚rure, se̚ruri, se̚rurii, se̚rerii, se̚rorisu* (Arakawa, p. 680 and p. 682), but in the end *serori* won out and is now the only version used.

Celery was imported to Japan in the second half of

the nineteenth century, and it was first cultivated in Japan in 1868 (Sanseidō, p. 376).

(1) Nihon de wa doko no yaoya de mo serori o utte-iru wake ja nai.

"In Japan, not all vegetable shops sell celery."

se¹ru セル (<serge)

Like *saaji* (see *saaji*), *seru* comes from English *serge,* but *seru* is for Japanese-style clothing whereas *saaji* is for Western-style clothing.

Umegaki (1975b, p. 195) has an interesting theory as to why *serge* became *seru* in Japanese. According to him, *serge* first became *se¹ruji,* but gradually the last syllable, *ji,* was dropped. In Japanese, different kinds of fabrics are referred to either as *ki¹nu* "silk" or *kinu-ji* "silk material," *asa* "linen" or *asa-ji* "linen material," *momen* "cotton" or *momen-ji* "cotton material," etc. Umegaki speculates that since *ji* (written in the character 地) in such compounds as *kinu-ji, asa-ji,* and *momen-ji* means "material" or "fabric," *ji* in *seruji* gradually came to be identified with it by false analogy. Thus the version without *ji,* i.e. *seru,* was born and eventually replaced the older version, *seruji.*

se¹tto セット (<set)

The most common meaning of *setto* is "set" in the

sense of "a collection of articles designed for use together," as in a set of china, or "a collection, each member of which is adapted for a special use in a particular operation," as in *a set of golf clubs.* Examples of this are ko⌐ohii-se⌐tto (lit. coffee set) "coffee service," ti⌐i-se⌐tto (lit. tea set) "tea service," di⌐naa-se⌐tto (lit. dinner set) "dinnerware set," etc. There are some non-loans with the same meaning, such as hi⌐to-kumi, hi⌐to-so⌐roi, and *is-shiki,* but *setto* is used just as frequently as these—or perhaps even more so—because it is shorter and simpler.

(1) Nakamura-san ga kekkon-suru kara, tii-setto o age-yoo to omou.

"Mr. Nakamura is getting married. I think I'll give him a tea service."

Setto has other uses, for which there are no Japanese counterparts. First, *setto* is a set in such sports as tennis, ping-pong, etc., as in

(2) Tsugi no setto wa boku ga katsu yo.

"I'll take the next set."

Second, *setto* means "setting the hair." Japanese *suru* "to do" is regularly added to form a compound verb meaning "to set the hair."

(3) Kami o setto-shite-moraitai n desu kedo.

"I'd like to have my hair set."

Third, *setto* means "set" in the sense of "a construction representing a place or scene in which the action takes place in a movie or TV production," as in

(4) Are wa hontoo no uchi ja nakute, terebi no setto desu.

"That's not a real house; it's a set made for TV."

sha⌈ttaa-cha⌉nsu　シャッター・チャンス
(lit. shutter chance)

Shattaa-chansu is a fairly new pseudo-loan made up of two older loans, *sha⌉ttaa* "[camera] shutter" and *cha⌉nsu* "chance," and means "the best moment to press the shutter."

(1) Ano hito no shashin o toroo to omotte, shattaa-chansu o matte-iru n desu.

"I'm waiting for the right moment to take a picture of her."

shi⌈biru-mi⌉nimamu　シビル・ミニマム
(lit. civil minimum)

Shibiru-minimamu is a pseudo-loan meaning "a minimum standard of living to be guaranteed by city governments for the citizens." The word was first created by the Tokyo Metropolitan Office in 1968 as part of its long-range goals covering all aspects of civilian life such as housing, transportation, and social security.

(1) Tookyoo-to ga happyoo-shita shibiru-minimamu ga chikai shoorai ni tassei-sareru to wa dare mo shinjite-inai.

"Nobody believes that the minimum requirements for an average citizen's life announced by the Tokyo

Metropolitan Office can be fulfilled in the near future."

By coining this modern-sounding word, government officials obviously tried to give credibility to their plans. Only the most gullible citizens, however, were taken in by that trick, I am sure.

shi⌈chu⌉u シチュー (<stew)

Shichuu means "stew," a kind of meat and vegetable concoction. Stew was introduced to Japan in early Meiji. In the beginning, it was known as *su⌈chu⌉u* (Arakawa, p. 614), but as it became a popular dish in Japan, the word was used by more and more people who did not know or care about the original English word. The older *suchuu* was gradually replaced by the newer *shichuu,* which is now the only version used. *Shichuu* also appears in compounds such as *bi⌈ifu-shichu⌉u* "beef stew," *chi⌈kin-shichu⌉u* "chicken stew," and *ta⌈n-shichu⌉u* (lit. tongue stew) "stewed tongue."

(1) Konban no okazu wa shichuu desu yo.

"This evening we're having stew for dinner."

shi⌈ito-no⌉kku シート・ノック (lit. seat knock)

Shiito-nokku is a pseudo-loan used in baseball to mean "fielding practice." *Shiito* in this case is used in the sense of "seat," i. e. "position," while *no⌈kku* in Japanese baseball means "hitting a fungo, whether it is a fly or a grounder." *Shiito-nokku,* therefore, means "hitting fungoes to fielders in their respective positions." No one seems to know where, when, and by whom this pseudo-loan was coined.

(1) Shiito-nokku ga owatta kara, moo sugu shiai ga hajimaru deshoo.

"Now that the fielding practice is over, the game should be starting any minute."

shi˥nnaa シンナー (<thinner)

Shinnaa refers to thinner for diluting paint, varnish, rubber cement, etc.

Shinnaa became a household word in the late 60's when *shi˥nnaa-a˥sobi* "playing with thinner" became popular among the young as the Japanese counterpart of glue sniffing. These youngsters poured thinner in polyethylene bags and sniffed the vapor to get high. This fad, which resulted in some deaths, became a serious social problem.

shi˥npa シンパ (<*sympa*thizer)

Shinpa is short for *shi˥npasa˥izaa* and is used more often than the full form. *Shinpa* has a very limited meaning of "a person who does not belong to the Communist Party but is sympathetic to it, giving it financial or moral support."

(1) Aitsu wa Kyoosantooin ja nai ga shinpa da soo da.
"That guy is not a communist but a fellow traveler,
I hear."

This *shinpa,* written in katakana, must not be confused
with the other *shi¬npa,* written in *kanji* (新派), which
refers to a particular theatrical troupe.

shi⌐rubaa-shi¬ito シルバー・シート (lit. silver seat)

Shirubaa-shiito is a new pseudo-loan coined about
1973 to refer to seats reserved for old people on trains
and buses. The seats themselves are not necessarily silver-
colored, although some are. In English, gray is the color
associated with old age (e.g. *gray hair* and *gray-headed*).
In Japan, on the other hand, silver is considered the color
for the aged. Thus there are new euphemisms such as
sh⌐irubaa-e¬eji (lit. silver age) meaning "old age" and
shi⌐rubaa-ki¬gyoo (lit. silver business) meaning "business
of selling merchandise designed for senior citizens" (Fukao, p. 199).

(1) Wakai kata wa shirubaa-shiito ni suwaranaide-ku-
dasai.
"Will young passengers please not occupy seats reserved for senior citizens."

Shi⌐rubaa-Ui¬iku シルバー・ウイーク
(lit. Silver Week)
The one week from the end of April until early May

is nicknamed *Go⌐oruden-Ui⌐iku* (lit. Golden Week) in
Japan because three national holidays are crowded into
that one-week period, thus giving the movie industry and
other businesses a maximum opportunity to make money.

The first week of November, which includes another
national holiday, i.e. Culture Day (November 3), is called
Shirubaa-Uiiku. The word *Shirubaa-Uiiku* was invented
by the movie industry (Sanseidō, p. 318), but it is not as
common a term as *Gooruden-Uiiku.*

shi⌐sutemu-enjini⌐aringu   システム・エンジニアリング
(＜systems engineering)

When the new science "systems engineering" was introduced to Japan, the plural ending, -*s,* was dropped as
is often the case with English plural nouns that have come
into Japanese (e.g. *slippers, stockings,* and *pajamas,* which
have become *su⌐ri⌐ppa, su⌐to⌐kkingu,* and *pa⌐jama,* respectively). Hence, *shisutemu* "system" instead of **shisutemu-
zu* "systems."

Shisutemu-enjiniaringu is such a long loanword that
it is often abbreviated. There are three ways to do it:
(1) to translate the whole thing into Japanese, i.e. *so⌐shi-
ki-ko⌐ogaku,* which is a combination of *so⌐shiki* "system"
and *koogaku* "engineering," (2) to translate only the
second half into Japanese, i.e. *shi⌐sutemu-ko⌐ogaku,* or
(3) to use only the initials, i.e. SE.

sho⌐oto-sho⌐oto　ショート・ショート　(<short short)

Shooto-shooto refers to a short short story, i.e. a very short story, much more condensed than the average short story. In Japanese, *shooto-shooto* has a connotation of a story with a witty ending. This category became particularly popular through Shin'ichi Hoshi's fiction (Jijimondai Kenkyūjo, p. 164).

Although, in English, both *short short story* and *short short* are used, in Japanese, **sho⌐oto-shooto-suto⌐orii* does not exist, probably because of its excessive length.

su⌐kai-pa⌐akingu　スカイ・パーキング　(lit. sky parking)

Land shortage is one of the most serious problems facing Japan. *Sukai-paakingu* is therefore a necessity. The word refers to three-dimensional parking, i.e. a building built for parking—not an ordinary parking ramp, but a fancy tower with a caroussel-type box that carries cars to higher tiers, thus making it possible to park twenty cars in the tower built on a piece of land that is barely large enough for two automobiles (Jiyūkokuminsha, 1976, p. 382). This is like parking in the air. Hence *sukai-paakingu!*

The first *sukaipaakingu* appeared in Tokyo in 1962.

su⌐ka⌐uto　スカウト　(<scout)

Sukauto generally refers to only one thing in Japanese. It means "the act of searching for, and finding, new talent either for an athletic team or for a firm in the entertainment world; or a person hired for this purpose." *Sukauto* also becomes a compound verb with the addition of *suru* "to do," as in

(1) Kanojo wa moderu datta n desu ga, sukauto-sarete eiga-joyuu ni natta n desu.

"She used to be a fashion model, but was discovered by a scout and became a movie actress."

su⌈ke⌉eru スケール (<scale)

In English, the question "Do you have a scale?" would normally refer to an instrument for measuring weight. In Japanese, on the other hand, if someone asks "Sukeeru ga arimasu ka (lit. Do you have a scale?)," he is asking about a ruler. *Sukeeru* in this case is the equivalent of *mo⌈nosa⌉shi,* a non-loan.

Sukeeru is also used with reference to size or extent, as in

(1) Kare wa itsumo sukeeru no ookii koto o suru.

"He always does things on a grand scale."

The non-loan equivalent in this case would be *ki⌉bo,* which is used just as often, if not oftener.

su⌈ki⌉nshippu スキンシップ (lit. skinship)

It looks fairly certain to me that *sukinshippu* is a

clever compound made from *skin* and *kinship,* but as to
who coined the word and when, no one seems to know.
One thing is absolutely certain, however: *sukinshippu*
is a well-known word in Japan whereas *skinship* is not
in America (if used there at all).

The definition of *sukinshippu* is also vague. The
word is defined variously as "skin relationship" (Jiyūkokuminsha, 1976, p. 1184), "affective education of
children through skin contact with the parents" (Sanseidō, p. 329), or "child rearing through the skin" (Arakawa, p. 599).

Decades ago, when Japanese mothers regularly
breastfed their babies, carried them around on their
backs, and even slept with them, "skinship" was never
an issue. Nowadays, however, all those old practices are
scorned as "old-fashioned" by young mothers, who give
their babies too little physical contact. Children reared
without skin contact, however, often grow up unsure of
parental love and even of themselves. Child psycholo-
gists and pediatricians who became aware of this started using the word *sukinshippu* about 1970 to emphasize
the need for skin contact between parent and child. According to Fukao (p. 230), it was Nobuyoshi Hirai, a
noted child psychologist, who first introduced the word
sukinshippu. She reports that Hirai himself had heard
skinship used by an American woman at an international
conference of the World Health Organization in 1953.
It may have been just a play on words on the part of

this American woman at that time, but it has indeed
become a household word in Japan!

(1) Nihon-jin wa yoku "sukinshippu" "sukinshippu"
to iu keredomo, Amerika-jin wa sonna kotoba wa
shirimasen yo.

"Japanese often speak of 'skinship,' but Americans
don't know any such word."

su⌐ko⌐nku スコンク (<skunk)

English *skunk* came into Japanese and yielded two
different loanwords: (1) *su⌐ka⌐nku,* meaning the animal
skunk, and (2) *sukonku,* meaning "a defeat in baseball
without scoring."

In English, *skunk* could be used as a verb to mean
"to defeat thoroughly in a game, especially while keeping an opponent from scoring," as in *We skunked them in
a crucial game.* Some Japanese must have heard the word
used that way, but must have by mistake introduced it
as a noun instead. Instead of **sukonku-suru,* therefore,
we say *sukonku* or even *su⌐konku-ge⌐emu* (lit. skunk
game) to mean "a game that stinks (*or* stunk)," therefore, "an ignominious shutout."

Sukonku nowadays sounds a little dated. Most
youngsters would probably prefer the newer *sha⌐ttoa⌐uto*
"shut-out."

(1) Mata sukonku de maketa ka!
"We were skunked again!"

su⌐kura¬nburu スクランブル (＜scramble)

Sukuranburu has two main meanings in Japanese. First, it means "an emergency take-off of interceptors performed in the shortest possible time," but this is a military term unfamiliar to most civilians. The other meaning is the one familiar to people living in big cities, i. e. "a system of traffic control whereby pedestrians at an intersection are allowed to go in any direction, even diagonally, at the same time." Scramble crossways, familiar in some big cities in the U. S. A., were first tried in Kumamoto in 1968 and then spread to other Japanese cities. This kind of intersection is called *sukuranburu-koosaten* (lit. scramble intersection).

su⌐kuranburu-e¬ggu スクランブル・エッグ
                                    (＜*scramble*d *egg*s)

Japanese-style scrambled eggs, which have Japanese ingredients such as rice wine, are called *i⌐ri-ta¬mago*. Western-style scrambled eggs, made with "Western" ingredients such as milk and baking powder, are called *sukuranburu-eggu,* without the past-participle ending, *-ed,* or the plural ending, *-s.* However, the full form, with these endings added, i. e. *su⌐kuranburudo-e¬gguzu,* is also used despite its length.

su⌈kura⌉ppu スクラップ （＜scrap）

Sukurappu has two meanings. First, "old metal to be melted and reworked." But this meaning is probably not as common as the other, i. e. "clippings from newspapers, magazines, etc." *Scrapbook* is *su⌈kurappubu⌉kku* in Japanese, which is sometimes shortened to *sukurappu* also.

Clippings are referred to more often as *kirinuki,* a non-loan, than as *sukurappu,* but a scrapbook is probably more often called *sukurappubukku* than *kirinuki-choo,* a non-loan with the same meaning.

(1) Shinbun no kirinuki ga ooku natta no de, depaato de sukurappubukku o katta.

"I bought a scrapbook at a department store because I have too many newspaper clippings now."

su⌈kuriin-myu⌉ujikku スクリーン・ミュージック

(lit. screen music)

Made-for-movies music is called either *e⌈iga-o⌉ngaku* (lit. movie music), a non-loan, or *sukuriin-myuujikku.* The latter is probably not as common as the former.

su⌈ku⌉upu スクープ （＜scoop）

Sukuupu expresses only one meaning in Japanese, i. e. "a news item revealed in one newspaper, magazine, newscast, etc., before others."

(1)   Kore wa Asahi no sukuupu da.

      "The *Asahi* pulled a scoop on this one."

Sukuupu is similar in meaning to the non-loan counterpart *tokudane,* but *tokudane* probably has a broader
range of meaning since it means not only "a scoop" but
simply "big news" as well.

Sukuupu with the addition of *suru* "to do" becomes
a compound verb, as in

(2)   Kootaishi-denka no gokekkon no oaite ni kanshite
      wa, dono shinbunsha mo otagai ni sukuupu-shinai
      koto o yakusoku-shita.

      "With regard to the Crown Prince's future spouse,
      all newspapers promised not to scoop one anoth-
      er."

su⌐ku⌐uringu   スクーリング (<schooling)

In English, *schooling* means "education received in a
school." Its Japanese counterpart is usually *ga⌐kkoo-
kyo⌐oiku* "school education." The loanword *sukuuringu*
is used in a highly specialized sense: "classroom instruc-
tion given to students taking a correspondence course."
At the end of a correspondence course, the students are
required to attend a specified number of classroom ses-
sions called *sukuuringu* in order to receive full credit.

(1)   Ato sukuuringu sae owareba sotsugyoo desu.

      "For graduation, I have only to fulfill the 'school-
      ing' requirement."

su͡kyu͡uba　スキューバ　(<scuba)

Sukyuuba comes from *scuba,* meaning "*s*elf-contained *u*nderwater *b*reathing *a*pparatus." Although *scuba* is pronounced [skúubə] in English, it has become *sukyuuba* in Japanese rather than **su͡ku͡uba,* which would have been closer to the original. The Japanese pronunciation indicates that the word was borrowed through the eye, and not through the ear. Since the country of Cuba is known as *Kyu͡uba* in Japan rather than **Ku͡uba,* someone must have decided that *scuba* too should be pronounced [sukyúuba].

Scuba diving is *su͡kyuuba-da͡ibingu.*

(1)　Konogoro wa Nihon de mo sukyuuba-daibingu ga kanari sakan ni natte-kita.

　　　"These days, scuba diving has become pretty popular in Japan, too."

su͡mairu-ba͡jji　スマイル・バッジ　(lit. smile badge)

Americans love to wear buttons with messages. For example, during an election campaign, supporters of a particular candidate wear buttons with his name on. In Japan, buttons sewn on clothes are called *botan* (from Portuguese *botão*), but buttons with messages are called *ba͡jji* (from English *badge*) instead. Although buttons of the latter type are not very common in Japan, Smilie buttons became slightly popular about 1966 (Jiyūkokuminsha, 1976, p. 1017) by the name of *sumairu-bajji.*

su⌈ma⌉kku スマック (lit. smack)

Sumakku or *a⌈isu-suma⌉kku* (lit. ice smack) is a pseudo-loan referring to a chocolate-coated, cylindrical popcicle. There is no non-loan counterpart. If I remember correctly, the word was first used in the mid-1930's.

(1) Furiizaa ni haitte-iru sumakku tabete mo ii?
     "May I eat the 'ice smack' in the freezer?"

su⌈mooku-sa⌉amon スモーク・サーモン
                                              (<*smoked salmon*)

Smoked food used to be known as *kunsei,* a non-loan, before World War II. For example, smoked salmon used to be called *sa⌉ke no kunsei.* Nowadays, however, the trend seems to be from *kunsei* to *su⌈mo⌉oku,* mainly because *sumooku* is easier to write in katakana and sounds more up-to-date. Hence *sumooku-saamon* "smoked salmon," *su⌈mooku-ha⌉mu* "smoked ham," *su⌈mooku-he⌉ringu* "smoked herring," etc. *Su⌈mo⌉oku* is short for *su⌈mo⌉okuto* "smoked," a more "correct" but less used version.

su⌈mu⌉usu スムース (<smooth)

In English, *smooth* is pronounced [smuuð]. In other words, the final consonant is voiced. Japanese speakers mistook it for a voiceless sound [θ] by misidentifying it with the final consonant in other English words ending in *th*, such as *tooth* and *booth*, and borrowed the word as *sumuusu*.

This loan is used only figuratively, in the sense of "free from hindrances or difficulties," as in

(1)   Banji sumuusu ni itte yokatta desu nee.

"Wasn't it nice that everything went smoothly?"

The more "correct" version, *su⌐mu⌐uzu*, is also used, but probably not as frequently.

su⌐pi⌐ichi   スピーチ   (<speech)

Supiichi is much more limited in meaning than English *speech* and usually refers to a particular type of speech, i. e. an after-dinner speech (Yoshizawa, p. 479).

(1)   Shokuji ga owatta tokoro de Yamamoto-sensei no supiichi ga hajimatta.

"As soon as dinner was over, Professor Yamamoto's speech began."

su⌐piido-da⌐un   スピード・ダウン   (lit. speed down)

English *speed up* meaning "to increase the rate of speed" came into Japanese and became *su⌐piido-a⌐ppu*, as in

(1)   Chotto okureta kara, supiido-appu-shimashoo.

"We are a little behind schedule; let's speed up."

By false analogy, a new pseudo-loan, *supiido-daun* was created in Japan as an antonym.

(2)   Kikai ga supiido-daun-shinai yoo ni ki o tsukete-
      kudasai.
      "Please keep an eye on the machine so it doesn't
      slow down."

In English, of course, there is no such expression as
speed down. One would say *slow down* instead.

su⌈po⌉iru-suru   スポイルする   (<spoil)

Supoiru, from English *spoil,* plus Japanese *suru* "to
do" constitutes a compound verb, *supoiru-suru,* meaning
"to spoil." *Supoiru-suru,* however, is much more limited
in meaning than *spoil.* Unlike *spoil,* which could be used
with reference to things (e.g., *The fruit was spoiled by
worms* or *The picnic was spoiled by bad weather*), *supoiru-suru* is used exclusively with reference to human beings
(and sometimes animals) in the sense of "to harm the
character of someone by excessive indulgence."

(1)   Ano ko wa hitorikko da kara, sukkari oya ni supo-
      iru-sarete-shimatta yoo da.
      "It seems that that child has been completely spoiled
      by his parents because he is an only child."

Supoiru-suru is different from *amayakasu* "to pam-
per" in that the latter does not necessarily result in harmed
character.

su⌈rii-e⌉su   スリー・S (lit. 3 S's)

Since the days of the *sa⌈nshu no ji⌉ngi,* i.e. the three

divine treasures associated with the Japanese imperial throne, the Japanese have always liked to talk about a set of three. One of the latest sets of three is *surii-esu,* referring to three items (the English names of which all start with *s*) that are supposed to be the three greatest necessities for modern man: *s*ex (or *s*peed), *s*ports, and *s*creen (i.e. movies) (Jiyūkokuminsha, 1976, p. 1312).

Another well-known set of three is *surii-shii* (lit. 3 C's): *c*ar, *c*ooler (i. e. air-conditioner), and *c*olor TV—the three items considered indispensable for a modern household.

su⌐rii-sa⌐izu　スリー・サイズ　(lit. three size)

Surii-saizu is a new pseudo-loan referring to a woman's bust, waist, and hip measurements.

(1)　Ano hito no surii-saizu dono-gurai kashira.
　　"I wonder what her measurements are."

Americans should be aware that Japanese measurements are given in centimeters. So if you hear about a woman whose measurements are 90-65-90, don't imagine an Amazon! That's just the metric equivalent of 36-26-36.

su⌐ri⌐raa　スリラー　(<thriller)

In English, one who or that which thrills is a thriller. For example, a very exciting baseball game may be called a thriller.

In Japanese, however, *suriraa* has a much narrower meaning, i. e. "a suspenseful story, play, or movie."

(1) Hitchikokku wa suriraa-eiga no kantoku to shite Nihon de mo yuumei datta.

"Hitchcock was well-known in Japan, too, for directing thrillers."

A baseball game, no matter how thrilling, may never be called a *suriraa* in Japanese.

su⌐ro⌐o-moo スロー・モー (<*slow-mo*tion)

Slow-motion shots are called *su⌐roo-mo⌐oshon* in Japanese, as in

(1) Ano eiga ni wa zuibun suroo-mooshon no shiin ga irete-aru.

"That movie has a lot of scenes where slow-motion shots were used."

There is a non-loan counterpart of *suroo-mooshon,* i. e. *ko⌐osokudo-sa⌐tsuei* (lit. high-speed shot), which sounds more technical.

While the full form, *suroo-mooshon,* usually refers to movies and videotapes only, the shorter version, *su⌐ro⌐o-moo,* is specifically used as a derogatory word for people who move slowly.

(2) Aitsu suroo-moo de komaru ne.

"That guy is so slow I can't stand it."

In all the loanword dictionaries I consulted, *suroo-moo* is explained as a Japanese abbreviation. As far as

I know, no scholar has pointed out so far that *slow-motion* is often shortened to *slo-mo* in English also, as a TV sportscaster might say, "Let's see that in slo-mo." The only difference between English *slo-mo* and Japanese *suroo-moo* is that the former is a TV/film term whereas the latter is not.

su⌈taato-ra⌉in スタート・ライン (＜*start*ing *line*)

The starting line for a race is a *sutaato-rain* in Japanese.

(1) Tsugi no reesu no sutaato-rain wa doko deshoo.
   "I wonder where the starting line is for the next race."

Obviously the *-ing* ending in *starting* was dropped when the word was borrowed into Japanese. No one therefore says **su⌈taatingu-ra⌉in*. There are other loanwords which likewise show the elimination of *-ing,* e.g. *me⌈jaa-ka⌉ppu* (lit. measure cup) "measuring cup" and *ha⌈ppii-e⌉ndo* (lit. happy end) "happy ending."

su⌈tando-pure⌉e スタンド・プレー (lit. stand play)

In English, *stands* is sometimes used in the sense of *grandstand*. It is not clear whether Japanese *sutando* meaning "grandstand" comes from *grandstand* or *stands*.

(1) Sutando no kankyaku wa moo hotondo kaette-shimatta.

"Most of the spectators in the grandstand have already left."

Since *grandstand* is *sutando,* and not *⌜gu⌝randosuta-ndo, grandstand play* is also *sutando-puree,* and not *⌜gu⌝randosutando-pure⌝e.*

(2) Ano senshu wa sutando-puree bakari yatte-iru.

"That player does nothing but grandstand plays."

Like English *grandstand play, sutando-puree* may be used figuratively in non-sports situations, too.

(3) Sutando-puree no suki na seijika wa iya desu ne.

"I don't like politicians who like grandstand plays."

su⌜te⌝eshon　ステーション　(＜station)

A loanword is sometimes replaced by a non-loan. This is rare, but it does happen. *Suteeshon* meaning "railroad station" is one of those few loanwords that have been replaced by non-loans. During the Meiji era, the loanword *suteeshon* was apparently a very common word, and even in early Showa, it was still alive and was occasionally used. Nowadays, however, the non-loan *e⌝ki* is probably about the only word used in the sense of "railroad station."

Suteeshon meaning "railroad station" is used only in compounds today, such as *su⌜teeshon-ho⌝teru* (lit. station hotel) meaning "hotel inside a station building" and *su⌜teeshon-bi⌝ru* "[railroad] station building."

su⌐te⌐kki ステッキ （＜stick）

When a walking stick was common in the West, it was also popular with Japanese men by the name of *sutekki.*

The fact that *stick* was borrowed into Japanese as *sutekki* rather than *su⌐ti⌐kku* shows that it was borrowed fairly early, as in the case of *bu⌐re⌐eki* "brake" and *ke⌐eki* "cake." Sanki Ichikawa (p. 199) points out that *i* was added instead of *u* "where the neighboring vowel was a front vowel like *e* and *i.*"

(1) Hito-mukashi mae no haikara-shinshi wa sutekki o motte aruite-ita.

"Trendy men of a while ago used to carry around walking sticks."

Sutekki implies walking sticks carried as a fad, whereas the non-loan *tsu⌐e⌐* refers to canes used by people with walking difficulty.

When carrying a stick was the fad, a new pseudo-loan *su⌐tekki-ga⌐aru* (lit. stick girl) was created to mean "a young female hired to accompany a man for a stroll." This pseudo-loan, however, is out of use today.

su⌐ti⌐kku スティック （＜stick）

Like *su⌐te⌐kki* (see *sutekki*), *sutikku* also comes from English *stick,* but this is a more recent loan meaning exclusively "a stick used in sports such as field hockey and ice hockey." In other words, the same English word has yielded two different loanwords in Japanese with two different meanings. There are other English words that have resulted in more than one loanword in Japanese, e.g. strike→ *su⌐to⌐raiku* "a strike in baseball" and *su⌐to⌐ra-iki* "a labor strike"; lemonade→ *ramune* "a kind of lemon-flavored soda pop" and *re⌐mone⌐edo* "lemonade."

Su⌐to⌐ppu-za ストップ・ザ (<Stop the)

In the 1930's, when Babe Ruth, Lou Gehrig, and the gang were at their peak, the New York Yankees were virtually unstoppable, and other teams vowed to "*stop the* Yankees."

For some reason, this slogan was introduced to Japan and provided the formula *sutoppu-za* to be applied to similar situations where there is a perennial champion whom everyone else wants to dethrone. For example, when the Tokyo Giants were invincible in the early '70s, other terms tried hard to "Sutoppu-za Jaiantsu," i.e. "Stop the Giants." *Za* became so closely associated with *sutoppu* that *sutoppu-za* unfortunately came to be recognized as one word. Thus, when the premiership of the late Prime Minister Satō ('64-'72) dragged on too long for his political foes, even within his own party, they vowed to "Sutoppu-za Satoo" (lit. Stop the Satō) instead of "*Sutoppu Satoo"!

su⌐tore⌐eto　ストレート　(＜straight)

English *straight* meaning "without a bend, angle, or curve" usually corresponds to Japanese *ma⌐ssu⌐gu,* as in *massugu na michi* "a straight road." The loanword *sutoreeto* has more specialized meanings. First, it means "undiluted," as in

(1)　Uisukii o sutoreeto de nomu no wa yoku arimasen yo.

　　　"It's not good for you to drink whiskey straight, you know."

Second, *sutoreeto* refers to a hand in poker containing five cards in sequence, as in

(2)　Hachi ga kureba sutoreeto ni natta n desu ga nee.

　　　"If I had gotten an 8, I would have had a straight."

Third, *sutoreeto* is a straight punch in boxing, as in

(3)　Joo Ruisu no sutoreeto wa sugokatta.

　　　"Joe Louis had a terrific straight."

Fourth, it refers to a high school graduate entering college without losing a year in between.

(4)　Yoshizawa wa sutoreeto de Toodai ni haitta.

　　　"Yoshizawa entered Tokyo University straight from high school."

Fifth, *sutoreeto* is a fastball thrown by a baseball pitcher.

(5)　Nooman Raian no sutoreeto wa jissai dono-gurai no supiido daroo ka.

　　　"I wonder how fast Norman Ryan's fastball really is."

In this case, *chokkyuu* (lit. straight ball), a non-loan, is used at least as often.

Sixth, in tennis, *sutoreeto* is a down-the-line shot, as in

(6)   Foa-hando no sutoreeto ga kimarimashita.
       "That was a forehand down-the-line winner."

Seventh, *sutoreeto* means "consecutive" in some sports situations.

(7)   Sutoreeto no yonkyuu de ichi-rui e.
       "He walks on four straight balls."

(8)   Ni-setto sutoreeto de kachimashita.
       "I won two straight sets."

su͏toreˈsu ストレス (<stress)

Sutoresu is used in Japanese only as a psychological term meaning "physical, mental, or emotional strain or tension."

(1)   Sutoresu ga kasanaru to noirooze ni naru.
       "When stress accumulates, it results in neurosis."

su͏toriˈppu ストリップ (<strip)

Sutorippu, from English *strip,* is used only as an abbreviation of *suˈtorippu-shoˈo* (lit. strip show) "striptease."

(1)   Konogoro sutorippu wa moo amari hayatte-inai.
       "Striptease is not very popular any more these days."

Striptease was introduced to Japan by the name of *sutorippu-shoo* or *sutorippu*. A stripper was called either *su⌐tori⌐ppaa* "stripper," *su⌐torippu-da⌐nsaa* (lit. strip dancer), or *su⌐torippu-ga⌐aru* (lit. strip girl).

su⌐to⌐roo ストロー (<straw)

A stalk of barley, rye, wheat, etc., is called *mu⌐gi-wa⌐ra* in Japanese, as in

(1) Mugi-wara de booshi o tsukuru koto ga arimasu ka.

   "Are hats ever made of straw?"

A tube for sucking a beverage, however, is called *sutoroo,* from English *straw.* Nowadays, of course, most *sutoroo* are either wax paper or plastic.

(2) Aisu-tii wa sutoroo de nomu to nomi-yasui desu yo.

   "Iced tea would be easier to drink with a straw."

su⌐upaa-ka⌐a スーパー・カー (lit. super-car)

Suupaa-kaa is a pseudo-loan coined about 1977 to refer to futuristic, high-performance European sports cars. For a while, all Japanese youngsters were talking about *suupaa-kaa,* buying model "super-cars" and collecting *su⌐upaa-kaa-ka⌐ado* (lit. super-car card).

su⌐upaa-suto⌐a スーパー・ストア (lit. super-store)

Suupaa-sutoa is a pseudo-loan referring to a self-service-type retail store dealing mainly in clothing and sundries instead of groceries. Picture books sold exclusively at *su⌐upaa-suto⌐a* are called *su⌐upaa-bu⌐kkusu* (lit. super-books) (Jiyūkokuminsha, 1976, p. 1018).

su⌐upu　スープ　(＜soup)

Suupu, from English *soup,* refers only to non-Japanese-type soup, e.g. Western, Chinese, etc. Japanese-type soup is either *mi⌐soshi⌐ru* "miso soup" or *su⌐mashiji⌐ru* "clear soup," both non-loans.

In Japanese, soup is something to be "drunk" (i.e. *no⌐mu*), rather than "eaten" (i.e. *ta⌐be⌐ru*).

(1)　Resutoran de suupu o nomu toki wa oto o tatenai hoo ga ii desu yo.

　　　"It would be better not to slurp when you eat (lit. drink) soup at a restaurant."

Until early Meiji, Western-style soup was called *so⌐ppu* (from Dutch *soep*). As the influence of English became stronger than that of Dutch, however, *suupu* gradually replaced the older *soppu*.

ta⌐aminaru-bi⌐ru　ターミナル・ビル
(＜*terminal buil*ding)

A building in which a railroad terminates is a *taaminaru-biru*. There is no non-loan equivalent.

ta⌐aminaru-depa⌐ato　ターミナル・デパート

(lit. terminal department store)

A department store located in a *ta⌐aminaru-bi⌐ru* (see *taaminaru-biru*) is a *taaminaru-depaato*. There is no non-loan equivalent.

ta⌐imu-a⌐ppu　タイム・アップ　(< *Time's up.*)

Taimu-appu is a term used in such sports as basketball and soccer to mean "Time's up." The *'s* in *Time's up* was dropped in the process of borrowing. Otherwise, we would have **ta⌐imuzu-a⌐ppu* instead.

(1) Ato ni-fun de taimu-appu desu yo.

"Time will be up in two more minutes."

ta⌐imurii-e⌐raa　タイムリー・エラー　(lit. timely error)

In baseball, a hit at an opportune moment is called a *timely hit,* which has become *ta⌐imurii-hi⌐tto* in Japanese. By false analogy, baseball-related people in Japan, probably reporters or announcers, coined *taimurii-eraa* to mean "error at a crucial moment." As Hani says (p. 56), English speakers would say "untimely error," but never "*timely error."

(1) Kyuu-kai no ura ni taimurii-eraa ga dete, makete-shimatta.

"We lost because of an untimely error (lit. timely error) in the bottom of the ninth."

ta⌐n タン (＜tongue)

Ordinarily, English *tongue* corresponds to Japanese *shi⌐ta⌐,* a non-loan.

(1) Byooki no toki ni wa shita ga shiroku naru.

"When one is sick, one's tongue turns white."

The loanword *tan* refers exclusively to the tongue of an animal (especially that of a beef) used for food.

(2) Kyoo wa nikuya de tan o katte, tan-shichuu ni shimashoo.

"Let's buy tongue at the meat market and make stewed tongue today."

The fact that *tongue* yielded *tan* rather than **ta⌐ngu* shows that the original word was probably learned through the ear.

te⌐eburu-se⌐ntaa テーブル・センター
(lit. table center)

Teeburu-sentaa is a pseudo-loan meaning "doily placed in the *center* of a *table* for decoration." Jiyūkoku-minsha (1976, p. 1304) explains that the correct English expression would be *centerpiece.* A centerpiece, however, is not necessarily a doily. It could be flowers in a vase, a candle stick, or some other work of art. The two words are therefore not synonymous.

(1) Teeburu-sentaa no ue ni nani mo okanaide-kudasai.

"Please don't put anything on the doily in the center of the table."

te⌐ema-myu⌐ujikku テーマ・ミュージック
(<Thema "theme"+music)

Theme music is called *teema-myuujikku* in Japanese, which is an odd combination of *te⌐ema* (from German *Thema* "theme") and *myu⌐ujikku* (from English *music*). *Teema* has been used in Japanese for decades, especially in such areas as music and literature, whereas *theme* never has. So when the new word *theme music* came into Japanese with talkies, it was only natural that *theme* was replaced by the already existing *teema* instead of yielding a new loan such as *shi⌐imu. Hence *teema-myuujikku.* There is a non-loan *shu⌐da⌐ikyoku,* which is a direct translation of English *theme music* and means the same thing. *Teema-myuujikku,* however, probably sounds more up-to-date.

There is a misconception in Japan that there is no such word as *theme music* in English. See, for example, Yoshizawa and Ishiwata (p. 353), who state that, in English, one says either *theme song* or simply *theme.* Of course, that is just a myth.

te⌐ema-so⌐ngu テーマ・ソング
(<Thema "theme"+song)

Teema-songu meaning "theme song" is a combination of *te⌐ema* (from German *Thema* "theme") and *so⌐ngu* "song." The word came about in exactly the same way as *te⌐ema-myu⌐ujikku* (see *teema-myuujikku*).

(1) Konogoro no eiga no teema-songu wa mukashi no
      hodo romanchikku ja nai to omoimasu.
      "I don't think theme songs in modern movies are
      as romantic as the ones in the old movies."
There is a non-loan *shu⌐da⌐ika,* which is a direct Japanese translation of the English. *Teema-songu* sounds
more up-to-date, however.

Te⌐kisasu-hi⌐tto テキサス・ヒット (lit. Texas hit)

Tekisasu-hitto is a baseball term meaning "Texas
leaguer, i.e. a blooper that drops between converging
infielders and outfielders." *Tekisasu-hitto* is sometimes
shortened to *Te⌐kisasu.*

(1) Kantan na furai ni miemashita ga Tekisasu ni na-
      rimashita.
      "It looked like a harmless popup but turned into a
      Texas leaguer."
Te⌐kisasu-ri⌐igaa "Texas leaguer" is also used but
probably not as often as *Tekisasu* or *Tekisasu-hitto.*

te⌐rasu-ha⌐usu テラス・ハウス (< *terrac*ed *house*)

Terasu-hausu is two-storied row houses, each with a
terrace, i.e. a paved area connected to the house.

te⌐ro テロ (< *terro*rism)

Tero is an abbreviation of *te⌐rori⌐zumu* (from English

terrorism). The shorter version, *tero,* is much more common than the full form.

(1) Saikin sekai-juu tero ga fuete-iru.

"Recently there is an increase in terrorism all over the world."

ti⌐sshu-pe⌐epaa　ティッシュ・ペーパー

(lit. tissue paper)

In English, *tissue paper* is a very thin, almost transparent paper used for wrapping delicate articles. Japanese *tisshu-peepaa,* on the other hand, usually refers to facial tissues, i.e. soft gauzy sheets of paper used for blowing one's nose, cleansing one's face, etc.

Tisshu-peepaa did not become popular in Japan until the '60s, when American-style tissues packaged in nice-looking boxes were introduced to Japan. Until then only unpackaged Japanese-style tissues were sold by the name of either *hanagami* (lit. nose paper) or *chirigami* (lit. dust paper). They are no longer very common.

(1) Uchi de wa konogoro chirigami ja nakute, tisshu-peepaa bakari tsukatte-imasu.

"At our house, we're using only American-style tissues these days, and not Japanese-style ones."

In America, facial tissues are often called "Kleenex" or simply "tissues." In Japanese, on the other hand, *ti⌐s-shu* alone often does not refer to facial tissues but rather to a fabric of light texture, particularly the kind woven with gold or silver. English *tissue* may also refer to that kind of fabric, but it has other meanings, as well.

to˺ppu-ba˺ttaa トップ・バッター (lit. top batter)

Toppu-battaa is a pseudo-loan used in baseball and means "leadoff."

(1) Kono chiimu no toppu-battaa wa dare desu ka.
    "Who is the leadoff man of this team?"

There is a non-loan equivalent, *se˺ntoo-da˺sha,* but it is probably not as commonly used as *toppu-battaa,* especially in speech.

to˺ppu-ku˺rasu トップ・クラス (lit. top class)

Toppu-kurasu is a pseudo-loan meaning "top level," "high-ranking" or "highest level."

(1) Ano kaisha wa toppu-kurassu ga minna roojin bakari desu.
    "At that company, the top-level executives are all old men."

to˺ppu-re˺dii トップ・レディー (lit. top lady)

Toppu-redii is a pseudo-loan with two meanings. First, it is used in the same sense as *fa˺asuto-re˺dii* "First Lady," i.e. the wife of the head of state, as in

(1) Amerika no toppu-redii wa daitooryoo-fujin de
aru.

"The First Lady (lit. Top Lady) of the U.S.A. is
the wife of the President."

Second, *toppu-redii* means "the foremost woman in
any field," as in

(2) Ano hito wa jibun o shakookai no toppu-redii to
omotteiru rashii.

"It looks as though she thinks that she is the lead-
ing socialite (lit. top lady in society)."

to⌐reeningu-sha⌐tsu トレーニング・シャツ
(lit. training shirt)

Just as sweat pants are called *to⌐reeningu-pa⌐ntsu* (lit.
training pants), a sweat shirt is called a *toreeningu-shatsu.* They are both pseudo-loans.

(1) Toreeningu-shatsu o kite hashitta kara hidoku ase
o kaite-shimatta.

"I perspired a lot because I ran with a sweat shirt
on."

tsu⌐na ツナ (＜tuna)

Tsuna, from English *tuna,* refers to only one kind of
tuna, i.e. canned tuna.

(1) Tsuna-sando o kudasai.

"I'd like a tuna sandwich, please."

Otherwise, *tuna* is *maguro,* a non-loan.

(2) Sakanaya de maguro o mi-kire kaimashita.

"I bought three slices of tuna at the fish market."

There is a non-loan *tsu⌐na⌐* meaning "rope," but that *tsuna* has an accent on the second syllable.

tsu⌐ri⌐i ツリー (<tree)

Tsurii is not an ordinary kind of tree. It is short for *Ku⌐risumasu-tsuri⌐i* "Christmas tree."

(1) Ano depaato wa Kurisumasu ni naru to ooki na tsurii o kazaru.

"That department store puts up a huge Christmas tree at Christmas time."

u⌐e⌐faasu ウエファース (<wafers)

Uefaasu comes from an English plural noun *wafers.* Even one wafer is usually called an *uefaasu* in Japanese, rarely an *u⌐e⌐faa.*

(1) Nihon no kissaten ya resutoran de aisu-kuriimu o chuumon-suru to, taitei uefaasu ga tsuite-kimasu.

"If you order ice cream at a coffee shop or a restaurant in Japan, it is usually served with a wafer."

According to Yoshizawa and Ishiwata (p. 77), the first Japanese wafers were manufactured by Fūgetsudō in 1891.

u⌐esuto-bo⌐oru ウエスト・ボール (lit. waste ball)

Uesuto-booru is a pseudo-loan commonly used in Japanese baseball to mean "pitchout."

(1) Ichi-rui-rannaa hashirimashita ga, pitchaa no uesuto-booru o kyatchaa ni-rui e nagete, rannaa auto.

   "The first-base runner ran, but the pitcher threw a pitchout. The catcher then threw the ball to second to get the runner out."

u⌐ezaa-o⌐oru ウエザー・オール (lit. weather all)

English *all-weather* has, for some reason, been reversed in Japanese to become *uezaa-ooru* (although o⌐oru-ue⌐zaa is also used sometimes).

(1) Uezaa-ooru-kooto o motte-iru to benri deshoo.

   "It would be convenient to have an all-weather coat."

Uezaa-ooru is the same as the non-loan *se⌐iu-ken'yoo* (lit. used for both sunny and rainy weather), but the former sounds more up-to-date and is therefore used by the garment industry.

ui⌐doo ウイドー (<widow)

The Japanese equivalent of *widow* is usually *mi⌐bo⌐o-jin,* a non-loan. The loanword *uidoo* is used only in compounds such as *go⌐rufu-ui⌐doo* "golf widow."

(1) Shujin ga gorufu ni kotte-iru no de, watashi wa
     gorufu-uidoo ni natte-shimaimashita.

     "Since my husband has turned into a golf nut, I've
     become a golf widow."

uˈuman-riˈbu ウーマン・リブ (lit. woman lib)

   Women's lib is *uuman-ribu* in Japanese. The reason
is that *uˈuˈman* has been used in some other loanwords
such as *seˈerusuuuˈman* "saleswoman" and *uˈuman-
paˈwaa* "woman power" while *uˈiˈmen* "women" has not
been a common vocabulary item in Japanese. When the
word *women's lib* came into Japan, therefore, the familiar
uuman replaced the unfamiliar *uˈiˈmenzu* "women's."

(1) Nihon no uuman-ribu wa Amerika no hodo sakan
     ja arimasen.

     "The women's lib movement in Japan is not as
     strong as the American counterpart."

waˈn-dan ワン・ダン (<one down)

   Wan-dan is a baseball term meaning "one down."
Although *waˈn-daun,* which is closer to *one down* in
pronunciation, is also used sometimes, *wan-dan* is probably more common because most Japanese find it easier
to pronounce. *Two down* is likewise *tsuˈu-dan* (or *tsuˈu-
daun*).

(1) Wan-dan, rannaa ichi-rui desu.

"It's one down with a runner on first."

Instead of *wan-dan,* one can also use other loan-words such as *waˉn-aˉuto* and *waˉn-naˉuto* (see *wan-nauto*), both from *one out.* In writing, a non-loan *is-shi* 一死 is frequently used because of its space-saving feature.

Strangely enough, in other sports such as boxing and football, *down* has become *daˉun,* not *daˉn.*

(2)　Mohamaddo Ari daun-shimashita ga, sugu tachi-agarimashita.

"Mohammad Ali went down but got up right away."

waˉn-naˉuto　ワン・ナウト　(<one out)

In Japanese baseball, *wan-nauto* (or *waˉn-aˉuto*) means "one out." Since, in English, *one out* is pronounced with a sort of liaison, *out* in *one out* sounds very much like [naut] to Japanese. Hence *wan-nauto.*

(1)　Wan-nauto furu-beesu desu.

"It's one out with bases loaded."

The funniest thing is that some speakers of Japanese have come to construe *nauto* (instead of *auto*) as a suffix meaning "out." These people thus say *tsuˉu-naˉuto* (lit. two *nout) instead of *tsuˉu-aˉuto* "two out"!

waˉn-saido-geˉemu　ワン・サイド・ゲーム
(<one-sided game)

English *one-sided game* should have yielded *waˉn-

saideddo-ge⌐emu, but it yielded *wan-saido-geemu* instead. The reason was obviously that **wan-saideddo-geemu* would have been much too long. The past participle ending, *-ed,* is often eliminated in the process of word borrowing from English into Japanese. Other examples would be *ko⌐on-bi⌐ifu* (<*corn*ed *beef*) and *ko⌐n-densu-mi⌐ruku* (<*condense*d *milk*).

W. C. (<W. C.)

W. C. meaning "water closet" in the sense of "toilet room" came into Japanese from British English. It is strictly a written form used for signs and blueprints. Although it is becoming an obsolete expression, some Japanese public toilets at out-of-the-way railroad stations might still have W. C. signs on the outside.

W. C. is pronounced [da⌐buryuu-shi⌐i].

zene-suto ゼネ・スト (<*gene*ral *st*rike)

General strike is *ze⌐neraru-sutora⌐iki,* but since *zene-raru-sutoraiki* is much too long, it is usually shortened to *zene-suto.* There are non-loans, i.e. *so⌐ohi⌐gyoo* and *do⌐omeihi⌐gyoo,* meaning the same thing, but the shortened loan *zene-suto* is easier to say and write and is therefore preferred.

BIBLIOGRAPHY

Arakawa, Sōbei (1975). *Kadokawa Gairaigo Jiten* (Kadokawa Loanword Dictionary), 44th edition. Tokyo: Kadokawa Shoten.

Bunkachō, ed. (1979). *Gairaigo* (Loanwords). Kotoba Series, Vol. 4, 5th printing. Tokyo: Ōkurashō Insatsukyoku.

Fukao, Tokiko (1979). *Katakana Kotoba* (Katakana Words). Tokyo: Simul Shuppankai.

Fukazawa, Yūsuke (1980). *"O-pea Monogatari"* (The Au-Pair Story), *Bungei Shunjū,* Vol. 58, No. 3, pp. 262-280.

Hani, Gyō (1977). *Chotto Ki ni Naru Supōtsu Eigo* (A Little Troublesome Sports English). Tokyo: The Japan Times.

Ichikawa, Sanki (1928). *"English Influence on Japanese,"* *Studies in English Literature,* Vol. 8, No. 2, pp. 165-208.

Ishiwata, Toshio (1976). *"Gairaigo"* (Loanwords), in *Gendai Nihongo* (Contemporary Japanese), ed. Takeshi Shibata, pp. 119-166. Tokyo: Asahi Shinbunsha.

Japan Foundation (1981). *Goi* (Vocabulary). Kyōshiyō Nihongo Kyōiku Handobukku (Handbooks for

Japanese Language Teachers), Vol. 5. Tokyo: Japan Foundation.

Jijimondai Kenkyūjo, ed. (1972). *Gendai Yōgo Jiten* (Dictionary of Contemporary Terminology). Tokyo: Shinsei Shuppansha.

Jiyūkokuminsha, ed. (1976). *Gendai Yōgo no Kisochishiki* (Basic Knowledge of Contemporary Terms). Tokyo: Jiyūkokuminsha.

Jiyūkokuminsha, ed. (1981). *Gendai Yōgo no Kisochishiki* (Basic Knowledge of Contemporary Terms). Tokyo: Jiyūkokuminsha.

Kashima, Shōzō (1981). *Japangurisshu: Gairaigo kara Eigo e* (Japanglish: From Loanwords to English). Tokyo: Santen Shobō.

Katō, Hidetoshi (1975). *Nihonjin no Shūhen* (Around the Japanese). Tokyo: Kōdansha.

Kōjien (1969). Ed. Izuru Shinmura, 2nd ed. Tokyo: Iwanami Shoten.

Kuze, Yoshio (1978). *Gairaigo Monoshiri Hyakka* (A Vast Stock of Information on Loanwords). Tokyo: Shinjinbutsuōraisha.

Miura, Akira (1979). *English Loanwords in Japanese: A Selection.* Tokyo, Japan, and Rutland, Vt.: Charles E. Tuttle.

Nihon Kokugo Dai-jiten (1976). Ed. Nihon Dai-jiten Kankō-kai, 2nd printing. Tokyo: Shōgakkan.

Nishio, Toraya (1979). *"Dōgigo-kan no Sentaku ni tsuite no Chōsa"* (A Survey of Selection Between

Synonyms), *The Journal of the School of Education, Gunma University,* Vol. 29, pp. 161-182.

Passin, Herbert (1978). *Enryo to Don'yoku* (Reserve and Greed). Tokyo: Shōdensha.

The Random House Dictionary of the English Language (1971). Ed. Jess Stain, the unabridged ed. New York: Random House.

Sanseidō editorial staff, ed. (1972). *Konsaisu Gairaigo Jiten* (Concise Loanword Dictionary). Tokyo: Sanseidō.

Ueda, Kazutoshi and Kanji Matsui, ed. (1969). *Dai Nihon Kokugo Jiten* (Dictionary of the National Language of Japan), 29th ed. Tokyo: Fuzanbō.

Umegaki, Minoru (1975a). *Gairaigo no Kenkyū* (A Study of Loanwords). Tokyo: Kenkyūsha.

Umegaki, Minoru (1975b). *Gairaigo* (Loanwords). Tokyo: Kōdansha.

Yokoi, Tadao (1973). *Gairaigo to Gaikokugo* (Loanwords and Foreign Words). Tokyo: Gendai Jānarizumu Shuppankai.

Yoshizawa, Norio (1979). *Zukai Gairaigo Jiten* (Illustrated Loanword Dictionary). Tokyo: Kadokawa Shoten.

Yoshizawa, Norio and Toshio Ishiwata (1979). *Gairaigo no Gogen* (Etymologies of Loanwords). Tokyo: Kadokawa Shoten.

INDEX

This index includes all the main entries as well as a few hundred more words that appear in the text explanations and the example sentences. The main entries are in boldface type while the other words are in regular type. Page numbers in boldface type show where the words appear as main entries. Accent marks are not used in the index.